THE AUTHOR

Michael Cooley was born in Tuam in the west of Ireland in 1934. He was educated at local Catholic schools and later studied engineering in Germany. In industry he specialised in engineering design and gained a PhD in computer-aided design.

Mike Cooley was national president of the Designers' Union in 1971 and a TUC delegate for many years. A design engineer for eighteen years, he was a founder member of the Lucas Aerospace Combine Shop Stewards' Committee and one of the authors of its Plan for Socially Useful Production.

He has lectured at universities in Australia, Europe and the United States. He has been a guest professor at the University of Bremen, and visiting professor at the University of Manchester Institute of Science and Technology. He has written for a variety of publications world wide including the *Guardian*, the *Listener* and the *New Statesman*. He has produced over forty scientific papers and is author or joint author of eleven books in English and German and has contributed to some thirty-five more. His work has been translated into over twenty languages from Finnish to Japanese. He is an international authority on human-centred computer-based systems and in 1981 was joint winner of the $50,000 Alternative Nobel Prize, which he donated to the Lucas Combine Committee.

Mike Cooley has been chairman and director of several manufacturing companies in his capacity as director of technology of the Greater London Enterprise Board in the 1980s.

His previous book, *Arhcitect or Bee? The Human Price of Technology*, was re-published by Spokesman in 2016.

DELINQUENT GENIUS

The Strange Affair of Man and His Technology

Mike Cooley

Foreword by

Michael D. Higgins

SPOKESMAN
Nottingham

Cover image: "What lies beneath" by Duncan Clarke, 2016, from the 'Landscape In Crisis' series, depicting neonicotinoidal insecticide molecules linked to honey-bee colony collapse and the loss of birds due to a reduction in insect populations.

First published in 2018

Spokesman
Russell House, Bulwell Lane,
Nottingham, NG6 0BT, England
www.spokesmanbooks.com
with the support of the Atlantic Peace Foundation

ISBN 978 085124 878 3

A cataloguing-in-publication (CIP) record is available from the British Library

Printed in the European Union

CONTENTS

FOREWORD

It is a great privilege to have been asked to write a Foreword for a book that I believe to be of the utmost importance for all those interested in advancing the debate on the recovered symmetry we do desperately need between science, technology, ecology and economics.

All of those, now in different generations, who are so impressed with Mike Cooley's *Architect or Bee?*, either in its original publication or its republication in 2016, will be deeply moved by the story of passion, intellectual curiosity, and deep social responsibility that is revealed in *Delinquent Genius – The Strange Affair of Man and Technology.* Mike Cooley may well be the most intelligent Irish man, the most morally engaged scientist and technologist Ireland has sent abroad. This book, however, was written during one of his periods of return to Ireland.

Professor Cooley has an extraordinary background. He is from a town in the West of Ireland which has produced, a playwright, Tom Murphy, regarded as the most poetic playwright of his generation. Mike Cooley, Tom Murphy and someone who would go on to be a leading trade unionist, Mick Brennan, were 'mates' anxious to make things, know how machines worked and invent new instruments. Towards that end they persuaded their parents to allow them to move from the more academic training of secondary education provided by the Christian Brothers to what was then called in Tuam *'The Tech'*.

The prejudice that is contained in the term *'The Tech'* is understandable in an economy with few employment opportunities. It was assumed that those born for a life in the labouring classes would find it an appropriate setting for their education. The professions, meanwhile, could draw from a different well.

What is extraordinary in the life, the work and the social contribution of Professor Cooley, and the others, is that they saw that excellence could be achieved through a combination of hand and brain, that curiosity was not an impediment to learning but rather a source of innovation. Even more importantly, they saw that the fruits of this collaboration and co-operation, of science and technology, of scholar and society offered the best prospect for a cohesive society and a dynamic economy.

Delinquent Genius – The Strange Affair of Man and His Technology is simply brimming with insights. It traces the sources of technology and its application. It is, above all else, a brilliant account of a dangerous hubris which can lead to that which is instrumental becoming a source, a dangerous source, of domination, of passive rather than active existence.

Elegant in its tracing of the sources of early achievements in architecture, for example, echoing a theme in *Architect or Bee?* it brings us from the Cupola of Santa Maria del Fiore right up to the 1990s using aesthetic and poetic references, where plain prose would be insufficient.

It is powerful in its reminding us of the life of the senses and of the consequences of a dominating artificiality that subverts the importance of experienced reality.

It is understandable that someone who was one of the earliest, most qualified scholars in design, who was national

President of the Designers' Union in 1971, and who, like his fellow schoolmate Mick Brennan, would value the importance of the collective in the trade union movement, would seek to bridge the gap between science and its application in the workplace through the hands of workers.

If this book was written for the 1990s it could not be more relevant in our present circumstances as the debate on the future of work, the impact of technology, sustainability and the perilous state of our planet gets under way.

I believe the publication of this book must be seen as an invaluable contribution. What is particularly moving in it is that it takes all of these issues that have been raised in different fora, and in different ways and locates them in a biographical experience of a brilliant scholar. There is something immensely hopeful in this, the sheer power that comes from retaining one's early curiosity, harvesting it through scholarship, and delivering it for the benefit of mankind.

The book offers a number of practical suggestions which are achievable. We must remember that, after all, its author served as Director of Technology for the Greater London Enterprise Board in the 1980s. Educationalists too can draw so much from it, as can those interested in spirituality, rather than the trading of certainties. A powerful case is made against the dangers of being one single source of answers and, above all, one single method.

We are reminded that we live in a binary age of great danger but also of great opportunities. From time to time the author turns to poets who anticipate the inadequacy of language in their distillation of the experience of the senses and the dreams of the future.

The author quotes an African leader who once said:

"Let your words be so clear and direct and simple that the ideas they represent flow through people's ordinary consciousness as easily and naturally as the wind and the rain flow through the trees."

Professor Mike Cooley, most brilliant son of Tuam and citizen of the world, has done just that in his beautiful book.

Michael D. Higgins
President of Ireland
October 2018

INTRODUCTION

This is the story of a very special relationship. It is one of the oldest and strangest in human history. It is almost as old as man himself. It has now developed into a relationship of terrible and all consuming passion. As in the best dramatic tradition, its consummation seems set to end in spectacular tragedy. It displays all the ingredients of a Greek tragedy but on a grand and universal scale. It is a drama which involves us all, both as actors and spectators.

The action centres on a perverse form of relationship in which one partner is the artificial creation of the other. As the story unfolds, we can behold a bizarre metamorphosis in which the artificial partner becomes increasingly real and the real partner becomes increasingly artificial.

The transformation of the partners is so complete that in some respects we can no longer tell them apart, so we have to devise tests so that we can identify which is which. We in the technologically advanced nations have been chosen by history for a front row seat at the final act of this spectacular. The plot so far suggests that the created is about to destroy its own creators.

There are those who say that this final act is already written, the stage props well and truly fixed into position and the outcome already determined. I disagree. I hope to show that the script for this finale can still be rewritten. This, I believe, is the greatest single task now facing humanity. It is no theatre of the bizarre but a real life drama in which the outcome will determine the future of humanity and the fate of our already wounded planet.

This 'life or death' drama is about the relationship between man and his technological toys. I do mean 'man' and not 'humanity', for it is a relationship from which women have been largely excluded and this to disastrous effect.

There are now many serious engineers and scientists who assert that the created is already surpassing its creator. The technological toys we have created are now so sophisticated, so elegant, so precise, so powerful, so 'intelligent', that they can surpass our own best endeavours, so these scientists casually refer to the human brain as the only computer built by amateurs.

They cousel us in sombre Darwinian tones: "Human Beings will have to accept their true place in the evolutionary heirarchy, namely animals, human beings and intelligent machines". This is a relationship gone seriously awry!

It all started out rather innocently with a little flirtation with primitive tools made from chips of flint. Then, man the hunter set off on his evolutionary journey armed with his favourite flint tipped spear, his inanimate partner in the chase. So it came about that a relationship which started out unpretentiously with the creation of rudimentary tools and devices has now ended up with the creation of machines of awesome complexity and earth shrinking power and vast systems which already dwarf us physically and are beginning to demean us intellectually.

Initially, the relationship was clumsy, hesitant and slow to ignite but man and his new partner, "my trusty sword", embarked on a journey which shaped the evolution of human society.

This book is a personal interpretation of the course of the relationship. It is in some respects a very ordinary story. In other regards it is quite extraordinary. It is ordinary because every human being who is alive today participates in it in one form or another. Most participate unconsciously. A minority agonise about the wisdom of the affair and some delight in the benefits it bestows upon them. It is extraordinary because it has led to a destination never visited by any other species; the end station being advanced technological society. Some nations and cultures have arrived there before others, but all of humanity, even in the most remote and unspoiled regions, are pursued with missionary zeal and are instructed that they must build and consummate the relationship or they are irretrievably lost. It is the path taken in the evolution of industrial man.

Timewise, it's been a very short journey in historical terms, a mere 30,000 years of "mood moulding, cycle wheeling history." Only our own species' arrogance makes it seem like an eternity.

The relationship has been at once glorious and disastrous. For most of the first 29,000 years, we still saw ourselves as part of nature. Our work patterns, festivals and cultures related closely to the seasons and to the flora and fauna around us. Things may have been difficult, but we were more in harmony with nature and as such, we did of course experience the hazards, difficulties and uncertainties in common with the fauna around us.

Only comparatively recently did we perceive ourselves to be above nature, which we increasingly saw as a mere resource to be controlled and exploited for our own ends. During the early stages it was clear from the species we encountered, that we ourselves were rather puny. We lacked the strength of the bear, the speed of the jaguar, the aquatic ability of the seal, the flight of the condor and the navigational ability of the salmon.

The one area where we seemed to have a headstart was our "smartness". Through our smartness, we evolved tools and implements together with organisational forms which allowed us to assert our dominance over the creatures around us. We became a tool-using species and as we fashioned tools, so in a subtle interaction we began to fashion ourselves to suit our tools. We extended the capability of our muscles with levers, screws and jacks; our energy with engines; our vision with telescopes and our voices with loudspeakers and communication networks. These machines and devices now stand between us and the physical world around us. They have become our hands, ears and eyes.

Over the past five hundred years, the speed at which we have propelled ourselves along this journey into technological society has ever increased and is now a ferocious velocity which appears to be out of control. It is this last 500 years which I hope to explore in this book. I would like to consider also those paths not taken, the alternatives that did exist and could still exist, but which we have tended to ignore. As a species we have become obsessed with exploiting and controlling everything about us. We cannot tolerate a species which surpasses us in any of its faculties. So we seek to evolve technologies which will always surpass their finest abilities. If we can't out-perform them personally, we evolve a machine which will do so on our behalf. So, armed with our chain saws and bulldozers, our ability to lob trees and build dams makes the eager beaver look like a hapless laggard. Our trains, cars and even motor cycles can casually outrun the jaguar; our planes outfly the condor and the swift; our Patriot missiles intercept Scuds in spectacular scientific displays which to some, makes the 'dive' of the peregrine on its airborne prey look somewhat feeble.

So we have been developing machines to do our bidding for us. With electronic tracking systems and vast dragnets, we use technology to fish the oceans for us in a grotesquely uneven contest in which, superficially, man appears always to be the winner. This is no longer the sustainable relationship of the hunter and the hunted, so celebrated in the North American Indian culture. With our vast earth-moving equipment and blasting techniques, we can now literally move mountains. Psychologically, we have become so arch interventionist that it appears as a lack of enterprise if we leave any area unchanged or the most remote wilderness firstly unexplored and then unexploited. As our machines become more and more sophisticated and 'active', so we as human beings become relatively more passive.

We could at least take refuge in the thought that although we were not developing much physically, we were certainly getting smarter and smarter. The scale and nature of our machines were, it seemed, a monument to our own intelligence. This was indeed seen to be progress. An essential part of our smartness was to design machines to free us from those heavy, laborious, tiresome, monotonous tasks and so we could become lazy to the point where it became necessary to contrive exercise.

Up to very recently, our machines tended to deal with physical work for us. Now however, as an extension of our smartness, we are developing 'smart machines' which will think for us and so we have evolved expert systems, artificial intelligence and neural-networking techniques.

In spite of the vast arsenal of technologies we have now assembled to act on our behalf, we have never as a species felt more insecure, disoriented and downright unhappy.

When our machine fails, when the power is cut, when the computer is down, we are suddenly very feeble again. We suddenly realise that we have lost many of our coping abilities and have been conferring life on machines and diminishing ourselves. We have in many cases become abject appendages to our own machines.

We have developed forms of education (more correctly described as training) which suit us to this mechanistic role. We have come to believe that the only things that really matter are those which have been discovered over the past seventy or eighty years. We have become mechanistic in a mechanised world. We are becoming highly sophisticated scientifically at a societal level yet dehumanised at a personal level. We have deluges of facts but little knowledge. We have now become far too smart scientifically to survive much longer without wisdom.

As a scientist and engineer, I too have contributed to the state in which we now find ourselves. I stand in awe of the wonders science and technology could bestow upon us, but I am horrified at what it is actually doing to our humanity and to nature and the environment.

So I should like to explore the route which has taken us to our present precarious state. What follows is not a whingeing description of the plight we have got ourselves into, deplorable as it may be. It is far more an attempt to trace the points at which we have taken false turnings, the opportunities we have missed and the constructive alternatives that will exist for forms of science and technology which will be caring of people and our wounded planet.

I shall attempt to show that there are real, exciting and human alternatives to the forms of science and technology that now surround us. I shall describe practical projects which I and others have been engaged upon and which lay the basis for that which I shall call 'socially useful' and 'human centred' products and systems. These are systems which enhance and celebrate human skill and ingenuity rather than marginalising it. They are systems which are 'amenable to the human spirit'. I shall also describe simple, practical products which would enhance the quality of our lives in an all-round fashion, but which at the same time, are ecologically desirable and environmentally friendly.

To demonstrate the need for such systems and products, I shall be describing and criticising the inbuilt values in modern science and technology. This will inevitably mean that I shall have to use some scientific terms, but I shall keep these to an absolute minimum for two reasons: firstly, it would make what I shall have to say difficult or perhaps inaccessible to many of my readers but secondly and more particularly, scientific terms and language are themselves part of the problem. Were I to write in the conventional scientific mode, I would simply be compounding the problem. Scientific language aims to be precise, exact and proscriptive. Indeed, that type of language is beginning to dominate the way we think and is beginning to be seen as the only way of expressing ourselves, when our society today urgently needs also the descriptive, that form of expression which can draw analogies, ones which resonate in our collective consciousness.

How does one describe in scientific terms, the loss of a loved one? We might try to say that the energy level of the grief was so many joules, but we all know what somebody means when they say they are heartbroken or devastated.

Likewise, how do we describe the sense of loss when a beloved valley is despoiled with a motorway, a familiar stream polluted or a childhood meadow no longer resounds with the sound of the corncrake? Artists, poets, painters and writers can always do this best because they call up those inner images which radiate meaning to us.

I hope I will be able to convey to the reader how I feel about these issues. Hopefully, my feelings may contact some kindred spirit in the consciousness of my readers. Part of the problem I will be discussing is a mechanistic form of behaviour in which we have been given to understand that feelings don't count any more. We are told that in the modern world we need facts not feelings. I shall challenge that view and attempt to show that we need both facts and feelings, the objective and the subjective, the intellectual and the manual, the male and the female, the qualitative as well as the quantitative. So I make no apology for intermingling images with facts, childhood impressions with hard engineering experience. Where a beautiful piece of poetry expresses more adequately, if less precisely than a scientific expression that which I wish to convey, then I will use poetry freely.

CHAPTER 1

THE CRAZED INTERVENTIONISTS

It is quite unspoilt. It is so unspoiled that its stands in reckless defiance of the missionary zeal of the technologist and the developer. Its naturalness and beauty would define it as underdeveloped. But underdevelopment is a terrible provocation to the massed armies of the crazed interventionists.

Like some partisan outpost yet to be mopped up, it still poses a threat to the surrounding forces. Its significance is both physical and emotional, for it stands as a potential rallying point around which alternatives may begin to form. It is a potent symbol of paths not taken. It speaks to us of other values and ways of doing things. Its apparent helplessness and vulnerability are deceptive. In its gentle and retreating way, it poses the greatest threat of all, the threat to our self image. Each nook and cranny whispers out that if we destroy it, we destroy ourselves. It tells those who will listen that we are not above nature and separate from it. We are part of it.

It is a sort of sanctuary, one of the few left in Europe. There is little outward sign that it has received the attention of the delinquent genius of our species. There are no interventionist scars made by the double edged scalpel of our technology. At this moment, there is not another human being in sight. No man made object, not even a house imposes itself. That great intrusion of our time, noise from man-made objects, is absent. There is no sound of transport, not even that of a car as it might propel some frenzied city dweller to temporarily probe the therapy of this place. No sound of an aircraft overhead as businessmen rush across the Atlantic to comsummate some multinational deal better left undone. The very absence of technology here invites us to think anew of its inbuilt values; values so well encapsulated in its own verbs: to "exploit" natural resources, to "manipulate" data, to "systematise" processes, to "control" nature.

This *carte blanche* landscape invites us to think how we might do things differently with the hindsight of recent experience. What forms of technology would be caring of nature and of human beings.

There is no noise here, but there are sounds, lots of sounds. A curlew calls like some woodwind in counterpoint to the harping of the sea and the kettledrum roll of pebbles on their well rounded way to dance a few more million years on the shores of time. A distant bird, perhaps a lapwing, performs an unselfconscious ballet in the dying light. The West wind comes freshly cleansed from the Atlantic's great scrubbing board.

But even here, the most unlikely messengers bring us unwelcome greetings from the realities of our times. That mystical wader, that unfailing winter visitor the woodcock, has arrived. On its route from Siberia, it has rested but a few days in Chernobyl-polluted Northern Sweden. Now in its extraordinary aerobatic flights through these Western seaboard hazel clumps, its tiny form carries two thousand becquerels per kilo. Its message penetrates, not only the sanctuary of this place, but also the sanctuary of our minds. It bring us messages of fundamental external changes which not only transform landscapes, but which will ultimately define what it is to be human. Here, the timescales of our development can be read more clearly than in any library. The humblest of creatures reminds us of the extraordinary brevity of our role on the stage of time.

The Burren is home to almost a hundred varieties of land snail. They make use of stores of lime laid down for them by their own marine ancestors some 350 million years ago. The Burren is fashioned in limestone, formed over a period of 350 to 270 million years ago. In the Burren's tapestry, we see the interwoven threads of a life. If like Greenpeace, we think of our planet's life on a scale of 46 years, then we as a species have been around for a mere four hours. During the last hour we discovered agriculture, and the industrial revolution began about a minute ago. It is only our own species' arrogance that allows us to confuse our brief latter day appearance with an eternity. Our existence has been short term and we behave in a short-term manner.

So, armed with our technology, we appear to stand as the masters of nature. We scramble fifty million tons of material around each year and in doing so, we shift the equivalent of three times the sediment moved each year by the world's rivers. We mine and burn billions of tons of coal each year, so venting those wastes, including carbon dioxide, the principal contributor to the greenhouse effect. Our agriculture is performed in such a way that we cause the erosion of 25 billion tons of soil each year, 0.7% of the total arable soil, soils which have taken thousands of years to form. We put down thirty kilograms of fertilizer per person each year to increase crop yield, so polluting the water we drink.

So chemical intensive has our agriculture now become that a recent report pointed out that in France, the milk from a mother's breast is so polluted it would be illegal to sell it in a bottle. Yet in the vernacular, in almost every language, we have terms such as 'as pure as a mother's milk'.

Our technology driven agriculture is already beginning to change our image of ourselves. It is also changing the environment. Above all, if we continue in the present manner, we will reduce by 50% all the species of flora and fauna in less that two centuries and this is more likely to be a matter of decades if we take the greenhouse effect into account. This will constitute a terrible reduction in bio-diversity, but it will also be accompanied by reductions in diversity amongst ourselves.

We are but ten years from the year 2000. That for me marks the end of an extraordinary millennium, a millennium which saw the decline of feudalism, the growth of our modern agricultural techniques, and the development of our cities in their present form; but above all it saw the development of our science and technology. So, I will seek to explore the last convulsed and exponential thousand years of our existence; to look at what beauty and what devastation we have wrought on our double edged way to the 21st century, to look at that journey in which we discovered the blessing and the curse of European technology.

On the journey these blessings and curses have included: the beauty of Venice and the hideousness of Chernobyl; Rontgen's X-rays with their vast medical potential, but which sprang from the same intellectual womb as the technologies we used to eradicate Hiroshima; the idealistic Diesel who hoped that his engine would bring prosperity to mankind worldwide but which powered the Panzers as they blitzkrieged the commencement of World War II.

I would like to explore, not so much what science and technology are doing to the environment. More eloquent and qualified voices than mine are addressing this issue. I would like to consider what we are doing to ourselves and to our humanity. Above all, I should like to make some modest proposals which might lay the basis for a human enhancing, liberatory technology and those industrial developments which are caring of nature and of ourselves. Our precarious situation cries out for a cultural and industrial renaissance, and there are already emerging the embryonic roots for such a flowering.

CHAPTER 2

THE ARTIFICIAL COMETH

There's something particularly sad about a person who loses their nerve. It is not so much the intrinsic state in which they find themselves, but rather that what is happening constitutes a deterioration. Tasks which they previously took in their stride now begin to seem impossible. The pilot who is afraid to fly, the surgeon afraid to operate, the nightwatchman afraid of the dark, the pedestrian afraid of the zebra crossing. The loss of nerve implied here, is a psychological fear of taking action rather than an inability to act based on, perhaps, ageing.

Those so afflicted are generally treated sympathetically. They are pitied, helped, supported and strongly encouraged with clichés of dubious value to pull up their socks, get their act together, face reality, take a break and get away from it all and we are assured that in no time, they will be as good as new. There are usually friends, institutions and professionals who will assist in the process of recovery. Temporarily at least, the person disabled through such a loss of nerve, allocates to others a major say in the running of their lives. But, what happens when a society as a whole begins to lose its nerve on an epidemic scale?

Our industrial society is now beginning to display all the ominous signs of such a degenerative malady. So pervasive is the loss of nerve, that we no longer believe in our own species' ability to cope with the problems that now confront us. Having long made a virtue of complexity, abstraction and quantification, we have gradually constructed an edifice of such labrynthine subtlety, such complicated codes and symbols, that we can no longer find our way through the maze we have created. So we seek in desperation, the comforting hand that will guide us through our self inflicted obstacle course. We cannot turn to other human beings since they are likewise confounded by the complexity of it all. So after years of weaning on that dangerous dependency in which for a thousand years we have conferred life on machines and diminished ourselves, we look to them, consciously or unconsciously, for our salvation.

For a thousand years, in a form of technocratic narcissism, we have been creating machines in our own image. The clockwork mechanisms and automata of medieval times, laid the basis for machines that 'walk', leading to the advanced robotic systems of today. From primitive steam engines, we have evolved energy transfer machines that 'feed', developing in size and power to life-threatening nuclear power stations. But above all, we have been developing machines that 'think', and so, intimidated into believing we can no longer think for ourselves, we turn to intelligent machines and artificial intelligence with the computer as the popular image of the flagship. It can store, collate and process vast numbers of facts way beyond the capability of our minds. It can process information at speeds so fast that we find it difficult even to conceptualise them. It can sift vast masses of data and extract new patterns and relationships. It is said that, properly programmed, it can even begin to arrive at novel solutions.

It is not so much that we are participating in these activities, but rather that we are witnessing them. They are external to us.

I shall describe subsequently, means by which such

systems can be designed to assist us rather than replace us. Here, I am simply attempting to describe a cult of the artificial, one which gradually denies us our direct involvement in processes. It also diminishes the significance of our own practical experience and knowledge. Above all, it is a situation in which the way we relate to our work, to each other – even to nature itself – is mediated by machines.

The machines stand between us and the world of activity and doing. Their graphic systems can give us powerful images of reality, but they are only images. Television may bring us beautifully filmed and presented material on plants and trees, but whilst this may extend our knowledge of these subjects at one level, it is not a substitute for actually feeling the texture of a tree trunk, smelling its leaves, climbing its boughs, feeling the weight of its material. Experiencing the day by day progress of its delightful blossoming in Spring and sampling the succulent sweetness or the face-grimacing bitterness of its Autumn fruit is a different level of knowledge. The TV image is less likely to inspire us to write poems about 'When I was young and easy under the apple boughs' or orchards being 'fair as the garden of the Lord to the famished eye of the rebel horde'. Even harmless ditties like 'Don't sit under the apple tree with anyone else but me' seem less likely if one hasn't been under an apple tree with or without someone else.

A dangerous metamorphosis is in progress when we begin to regard the artificial as more important than the real; or, worse still, if we begin to be incapable of making a decision as to which is the better since we cannot recognise one from the other. Cultural and technological developments over the last ten years are rapidly driving us in that direction.

It has certainly been a great decade for the artificial. Plans were laid, funds were granted, projects started and predictions were made that the artificial, in particular, artificial intelligence, would intrude into every area of our lives, even the most intimate. Connoisseurs of the image of the artificial argue which years will prove to be the vintage ones. 1983 must clearly be a frontrunner. An experienced taster would undoubtedly relish the following.

The ultimate house, we were assured, would be a structure which embodied a computer brain. It would be equipped with senses, and would be linked through telecommunication networks, with computer banks and, in case we thought it lacked a sense of community, with the brains of other houses. The house would of course be conscious, and would develop an awareness of its own existence. In case we regard this as impersonal, we should add that it would have an intimate knowledge of its inhabitants. Above all of course, it would communicate with them and we are reassuringly told that "once your house can talk to you, you may never feel alone again".

1983 was strong on compassion. The geriatric robot gives a flavour of the year's strengths. The geriatric robot is not hovering in the background like a vulture, waiting to grab your money and its own inheritance, nor, it is pointed out, will it slip a little something into your food to speed the inevitable. This electromechanical Florence Nightingale will not just minister to our physical needs such as bathing us and feeding us. It is also a companion which caters for our intellectual and psychological needs by listening. It is capable of asking us to tell it yet again about how wonderful, or how awful, our children and friends are to us. It urges us to please tell again our favourite stories and it never tires of hearing them because our favourites are its own favourites.

Yes, 1983 was all embracing in many senses of the word. We were informed that we could expect to see computers mature into an "intimate technology" and electronic sex was but a program away. Just as with all previous forms of technological change, it is justified on the basis that it will free us from routine, boring tasks and leave us free to engage in more creative activities. And so, in the case of electronic sex, a sequence of ministrations ordinarily requiring two hands, would be carried out automatically, allowing the lover to lavish attention elsewhere, just as one can set up rhythms on an electronic organ.

One may feel that 1983 is unassailable, but this would be a premature judgement. Although 1984 did not quite live up to its full Orwellian potential, it was no slouch in the artificial stakes. *Animal Farm*-like creatures of a more endearing nature had however emerged. There were robot dogs for the lonely and the threatened. They would bark when the doorbell rang, and the barking sequence was of varied form and duration to impress a would-be intruder. The more intelligent 'breeds' could in addition emit snarls and growls of chilling Baskerville ferocity. For the space conscious of those aspiring to greater things, there were little dogs with big barks. The choice of breeds and colours would satisfy most tastes and your dog would be good company for it never sulked and was, as one ad put it, free from the unpleasantness of 'ordinary' dogs for it would never need to 'go walkies'. There would of course be no emotion-charged, poem inspiring dramas of a Gelert kind. Viewed superficially, the year might be seen as one of harmless Pinocchio-type gadgetry, but there was a more sinister side.

In 1984, there were already students who had absorbed this culture of the artificial so satisfactorily that they thought of themselves as 'feeling computers' and as 'emotional machines'. If I were an arid quantifier who took refuge in numbers, 1985 might even have been special because some

5000 delegates registered for the International Joint Conference on AI in Los Angeles.

For me, 1985 was special because the artificial began to subsume the ordinary. It was that the artificial had passed a sort of horticultural Turing test. Turing had told us that a computer would be behaving intelligently, if it were in another room and as we communicated with it and received its responses, we would not be sure if we were communicating with a computer or with a human being. A horticultural Turing test is when we would view a flower and not know if it were real or artificial. Mrs June Tregale won a Gold Award at the Hollington County Show Devon, for her creation of an entire English Garden in plastic and silk flowers.[7] So good was the exhibit, that Mrs Tregale was compelled to declare "My biggest problem was the public, half of them could not believe the flowers were fake". Such a mistake is of course only possible if we fail to view something in its holistic sense. In this case there were only two levels of analysis – shape and colour. Had one added just one other level – smell, the artificial would have been seen for what it was.

The real and the artificial can be confused if we take objects out of their context. We are moving into a contextless world, one sadly devoid of a sense of place. We could hardly be confused by the flowers in the Burren which will assess with extraordinary capability, the time of year and the related temperature and climate at which they should emerge from the ground to make an entrance on the multicoloured landscape. There would be no confusion with the artificial when a Burren flower initiates the modest retreat of its outstretched petals as night approaches or the energy absorbing spread of those petals in the presence of sunlight. Its response to the winds are likewise indicative. Its gentle waltz in a soft caressing wind or a frenzied mazurka when the tree-uprooting gales blow. That great little navigator the bee, would not mistake Mrs Tregale's creations however good and beautiful, for the nectar-sweet secrets of the real thing. Mrs Tregale's garden can never be a 'bee loud glade'.

In 1988, the cult of the artificial had so subsumed the consciousness that not only did people believe that the artificial intelligence in machines made these machines human, but they also thought that they themselves were computers. This became a recognised psychiatric ailment, and psychiatrists in Canada worked on therapies to deal with it. Some of those afflicted were incapable of taking actions unless they instructed themselves in a form of machine code, or at least a precise programmed instruction. Like computers, they could not tolerate ambiguous instructions or imprecision of any kind, and when the psychiatrist asked one of the patients entering the consulting room to take a seat, he barked back "which seat"!

It's not yet clear how 1990 will fare, but it has made a strong start. It may well be remembered for introducing the concept of High Tech Grief in a manner which may yet give another meaning to "Finnegans Wake". In Japan, busy businessmen and politicians can now pay their last respects to a colleague by closed circuit television. The idea of the satellite funeral arose when Mitsui, the huge trading company, hired satellite time and transmission equipment to broadcast the funeral service of one of its senior advisors on closed circuit television. Together with a communications company and a funeral equipment wholesaler, the consortium is now beginning to sell the broadcast funeral in earnest. For 8 million yen (approximately 30 thousand pounds), they will set up two cameras and six large satellite monitors and beam an hour of satellite funeral service to locations across Japan. It is said that enquiries are brisk, and that of the 790 thousand Japanese who died in 1988, 100 thousand of them, all men of course, were the kind who could benefit from such a corporate television funeral. We know the Americans do their best to keep abreast of their Japanese competitors. In Las Vegas they have introduced drive-in funeral parlours where you can pay your last respects on a video-link without getting out of your car.[6]

So it is clear that the artificial takes many forms and guises, not just from the cradle to the grave, but even from pre-conception to the grave. I am not suggesting that the artificial and artificial intelligence has no useful human enhancing applications. It does, and I shall describe some of those applications in this book.

Nor am I suggesting that the artificial is some kind of bolt out of the blue. Throughout our development as a species, we've had paintings and icons and statues that were images of reality. We had stories, plays and poems contriving artificial situations which stimulated and enriched our imaginations. It is not that dimension of the issue I am addressing here, I am talking about a cultural outlook which has begun to put the artificial before the real, and regards intelligent machines as more significant than human beings: an outlook in which computer scientists can sneer at the human brain as "the only computer made by amateurs". It is a culture in which we are told that human beings will have to accept their true place in the evolutionary hierarchy namely, animals, human beings and intelligent machines.

Indeed, the zealots of the artificial intelligence research community now go further. At the British Computer Society's conference on Artificial Intelligence in Brighton in 1988, I spoke at a very well attended fringe meeting organised by the journal *AI and Society*. I spoke of the possibility of human centred systems which would be so designed as to provide powerful support tools for the most precious asset any society has, which is the skill, ingenuity and creativity of its people. I gave practical examples of systems which already do this in the context of the EEC ESPRIT Programme. I spoke about human creativity and intentionality and emotion and commitment.

The zealots accused me of being an 18th Century romantic (they were not kind enough to refer to me as a 20th Century romantic). They suggested from the floor in a sober exchange of ideas, that I should have the 'courage' to take seriously the notion that the real evolutionary element is not biological at all, it is something much more elusive namely 'intelligence'. Furthermore, I should admit that it is possible to identify in an historical analysis, that 'intelligence' allows a species to host it until that species becomes a liability. When this happens, when it is incapable of further development, 'intelligence' migrates to other species. The last biological species that intelligence has allowed to host it is the human species, but it has now recognised that species as a liability and is about to migrate to intelligent machines.

Many computer scientists now talk about the need to so design the future generations of AI systems that they will look after us and care for us and pamper us. The past decade has seen all these issues surface in quite blatant and open forms. I will seek to explore the historical background which has given rise to this form of technocratic culture, and also to explore the implications it has for us. Debates already exist in the scientific and academic communities, challenging this cult of the artificial and demonstrating that there are alternatives. What however is of deep concern, is that one of the historical tendencies of technological change is to render human beings passive and the systems active.

This is no accident. We have devloped our technology in this manner for very good reasons. Because of our frailty, we had to devise weapons to defeat more powerful animals. A capacity desirable at one historical stage has now reached such awesome proportions that in threatening our opponents, as with nuclear weapons, we also threaten ourselves. The notion that should limit these developments is not now seen as retrogression. On the contrary, it is seen as essential for human progress. Our relative weakness in a physical sense, stimulated our ingenuity in the design of our basic machines to multiply our strength, but 'labour saving' can so easily mean 'human displacing'. Our 'laziness', our praise of idleness, once such a stimulus to creativity, may well be reaching counter-productive proportions, for when we hand over more and more to our machines, including intelligent machines; when we get them to represent us, we so often position them between us and the real world of visual, audio and tactile feedback. Like the ancient Siren, the attraction of freedom from the physical is almost impossible to resist. In consequence, we are increasingly satisfied to accept that second order reality. Since we have less access to or experience of the practical, physical world around us, with all the subtle knowledge we absorb from it through all our five senses, we tend to deal more with models of reality than with reality itself.

The artificial is seldom presented to us in a context, or in any holistic way. If reality is just presented to us in narrow, fragmented, artificial forms and as a set of disconnected images, we cease to know the reality itself. This situation is now beginning to extend to our relation to nature. In consequence, there is a lack of respect for nature since it is so difficult to respect something that one does not know and cherish. So for me, 1985 was truly special. Not because more funds were lavished on artificial intelligence research than in any previous year, or because there surfaced more PhD's in AI topics, having made their "original contribution to knowledge" than in any previous year.

CHAPTER 3

ALL THE WORLD'S A FACTORY

"All the world's a stage and all the men and women merely players" according to Shakespeare's evocative theatrical analogy.

If that were appropriate in the 16th & 17th Century, it is certainly not appropriate today. Now, all the world's a factory and all the men and women merely units of production. Furthermore, all that surrounds us, be it flora, fauna or mineral, solid, liquid or gas is seen as raw material for technology's all-consuming factory.

We should of course give credit where credit is due and graciously admit that man has been fiendishly ingenious at the mass production of goods, even if they are in the main of a throwaway kind. They are usually the end result of highly sophisticated production technology and an outrageous and cretinous wastage of energy and materials.

Even if the product is primarily edible, this still tends to hold true. Witness the seemingly modest, but high tech quarter pound package of cheese slices. Let us for simplicity's sake, ignore the automated processing of the cheese itself. Consider just the latter stages of the production. Six wafer thin slices are prepared and each is enclosed in its own transparent plastic wallet with a flap which can be opened for ease of removal. Consider the delicate task involved here, even if one attempted to enclose the delicate wafer with dextrous human hands, well acquainted with the task.

The six enclosed slices are then placed in a neat bundle and sealed in an airtight transparant enclosure. These in turn are stacked in 50s or l00s in a close fitting carton suitable for transport. Imagine for a moment, the complexity of the special purpose machinery, the automatic control systems, the optical sensing devices and the conveyors which move each section from one part of the process to the other. This is all achieved automatically, untouched by human hands and results in hundreds of tons per week. Each slice, each package, each carton will be automatically quality controlled.

When next you visit a supermarkct, do look anew at one of these and imagine the complexity of the processes that led to it being presented to you on the shelf in that form. You might of course simply wonder why it is not adequate to straightforwardly buy a block of the cheese and apply a little bit of manual dexterity and also obtain a tactile feedback by slicing it yourself. As a technologist, I marvel at the ingenuity of the designers of such equipment but I also admit to being alarmed at the long term consequences of such a design philosophy and the priorities it sets itself. What we all need to consider is how the skill and ingenuity in these processes and techniques could be redirected from the present 'trivialities' and transformed into socially useful, sustainable production techniques.

There are however, much deeper and much less obvious issues which we have to address before our society can begin to redeem itself from the follies on which it is now embarked. That is, to explore why it should be that the factory model now so dominates our thinking and transforms more and more of our activities into production line-like routines.

Initially, society used to think of factories in the familiar terms of steel mills or Ford-like production lines in the automotive industry. The factory model has spread plague-like from these more obvious starting points to become an all pervasive model of how we should organise ourselves and our work.

It does not require great analysis to reach this conclusion. We need only look at a modern technology and chemical-intensive farming. The field will be organised like a factory layout. Gaps between the rows of crops reflect the width of the vast agricultural machines and the spread of their overhanging arms. The plants or seeds will have been inserted in a regular pattern in the ground by machinery. Huge combine harvesters will collect it and take the yield to high energy drying silos where it will automatically be conveyed up from hoppers and through the drying cylinders.

The egg production techniques for battery hens is another vivid example. Prescribed spaces, regulated heat and food input, maximum growth rate (quantity of course, before quality) and conveyors that transport the eggs away to be sorted into pre-determined categories. Thus it is with crops and with chickens.

The factory model now extends to a whole range of human activities. A modern city can well be understood and explained in terms of a factory model. Conveyors, which we usually call escalators or lifts, transport the units from one level to another. Transport systems of diverse kinds carry the unit to its point of production. Entry passes, predetermined entry codes and operator numbers allow the units into the appropriate place for their functioning. For many who dwell within the city, high rise flats (not homes) provide them with their storage space.

The factory model applies to most hospitals. Even for the most rewarding experiences such as childbirth, there is a factory environment of noise, high tech, flashing lights and lack of privacy. Maternity wards are frequently referred to by women in London as sausage machines.

Hotels have guest processing, computer controlled systems which are the real power behind the smile of those at the reception desk. There are pros and cons to the application of the factory model in these domains. Their consequences are reasonably obvious and therefore open to question, re-examination and modification.

These examples so far relate to the factory model being applied to physical activities. What is far more insidious is when it is applied within the cultural and educational domains. The dream of the technologist is now being applied to education at all its various levels.

This should of course, not come as any surprise to us. That doyen of production technology, the creator of production-line techniques which even Charlie Chaplin could not accurately parody, was shockingly honest about his plans for education. Henry Ford, when providing funding for a new form of education institution said, to the acclaim of his listeners: "I have tired of the production of automobiles to the point where I now wish to produce people. Standardisation will be the name of the game."

Standardisation has been one of the pinnacles of achievement for the production technologist. In its perfected form, each mass produced product is quite indistinguishable from another. The product is completely interchangeable with another product in the same range. More particularly, each component within the product is interchangeable with the components in other products in the same range. Every stage in the process is carefully geared to the grand finale – the truly standardised, interchangeable product.

Even before all this, there are the computer-based, goods-in quality control procedures (unknown to amateurs like Brunelleschi, Leonardo, Michelangelo, Manton and Chippendale, who naively believed you produced quality, not controlled it!), will ensure that all the incoming components and materials for performance compliance, dimensional tolerance and material integrity and are certified accordingly. Anything better than the standard acceptable is a highly reprehensible resource wastage, and a slight embellishment as much a deviation as a defect. Anything lower than the standard earns a reject ticket and consignment to the waste tip or in some cases reworking. The window of acceptance is a narrow slit indeed. Not great, not bad but just right, is the philosophy.

Above all, the component shall have absolutely no individual distinguishing features save that of the inspection number. Sameness becomes the hallmark of quality, interchangeability the passport to success. To ensure such crushing compliance even the initial formation of the component materials (its childhood if you like), right back to the initial process of the raw materials at the solid state physics level is required, and thus we have in-process quality control, inspection, testing, monitoring, classification and certification.

As a former senior design engineer in the Aerospace industry I need no lectures from my fellow technologists on the need for such ruthless compliance and conformity; rooted as it is in the cannon laws of predictability, repeatability and mathematical quantifiability! I am deeply aware that the lives of millions of my fellow citizens depend upon the exactness with which we carry out our stress analysis of structures, physical and performance testing of materials, test and quality procedures, and the meticulous adherence to predetermined approved procedures by skilled manual workers who produce the components, assemble them, and maintain these wonders of modern engineering.

These engineers and skilled manual workers display a deep professional responsibility, aware that any slight deviation, any hint of negligence will unleash consequences more catastrophic and more visible than similar lapses on the part of perhaps medical practitioners or surgeons. I am therefore not here questioning the significance or need for these procedures within their own domain. However arising from this, I do wish to raise a much more profound question. That is to say whether it is correct to elevate these narrow, technocratic, specific procedures to universal principles for the organisation of our society. More directly put, I wish to question that day to day metamorphosis which is transforming our society into a factory!

To those who charge that I exaggerate, I ask no more than that they look around them with eyes that see and listen to what is being said with ears that hear. I realise that a few swallows do not make a summer. I therefore cite the following not as isolated phenomena but rather as vivid examples of categories of developments which highlight the mechanisation of our society.

Throughout our history, universities have been regarded, rightly or wrongly, as an indicator of the level of our civilisation. As centres of learning they were held to embody some of the highest aspirations of our humanity: the transmission and development of culture, the pursuit of knowledge, the sanctuary of academic freedom and expression. In an all round way, they were regarded as institutions which reflected the highest cultural values of our societies.

I have described elsewhere that universities are now being organised on the model of the factory. In this model, students are referred to as commodities, examinations as quality control procedures and graduation as delivery. The professors are referred to as operators, sadly, an appallingly accurate description of some of those who now populate university faculties. There is even a computer-based, Frank-Wolf algorithm to work out the rate at which they are performing.

In all civilisations, those who provide caring curative services are highly regarded, at least in the rhetoric. Furthermore, to refer to somebody as a caring person is a form of praise, not abuse. These attributes were frequently regarded with justification as being female attributes and were highly regarded if sometimes lowly rewarded. Since the time of Florence Nightingale, many regard nursing as reflecting these values. Now however, as vividly pointed out by Ingela Josephson, the Swedish researcher in her seminal papers, nurses are to be transformed into engineers! What they do and the manner in which they care for patients must now be expressed and carried out with engineering and scientific precision. Nurses were informed as far back as 1976 by Robin Parsons (Josephson, *On Science and Knowledge* – the principle of a nursing college), that "The nurse must, once and for all learn to express her professional knowledge in exact terms. She cannot satisfy the demands of future technology by using a vocabulary that has become part of the tradition of nursing. Imprecise abstract terms, such as "loving care", "better patient care" and "caring for the whole person", are meaningless to computer technicians. They expect a nurse to be able to describe these concepts in a logical, scientific way using a vocabulary that is free from the clichés and the esoteric rhetoric that is part of her traditional vocabulary. Her descriptions must show how the result of her care can be measured quantitatively and evaluated. There are still those in our society both men and women who will not accept that loving care is a cliché and esoteric rhetoric. As Ingele Josephsen points out, love is expressed in action but becomes trivial when defined in scientific language to which it is not suited. However as in our factory model above it is assumed that these attributes can only be made really relevant if they are quantifiable and interchangable so a Finnish/Swedish professer in health care stated: "It is important to be able to give intellectual and spiritual content to the word 'Love' so that it may be understood and applied in the same way by different people". What we find surfacing secretly, surreptitiously, is once again the notion of exactness. We are back to Leibniz's plan to create a logical language with the certainty of mathematics; a language which would encompass all areas of human problems, particularly metaphysics, theology and ethics. He said on one occasion "Let us calculate, for this is the way that all religious and philosophical disputes may be mastered".

This thinking pervades our society at every level down to the most banal. The production line model applies likewise to the production of film scripts, so if *Rambo 1* accords with production and marketing requirements why not then have *Rambo 2* and *Rambo 3*? and so indeed we do.

All of this gives rise to that which is delightfully referred to as a human resource development problem. The trade union leader, Bill Attley (*Irish Times* Friday June 6th 1990) pointed out "Personnel Managers are now referred to as Human Resource Managers – which I find offensive. People are treated as machines, and they are like the maintenance managers".

The problem of human resource development is to produce people who are competent enough to do their jobs, but not bright enough to question what is going on around them in this narrow, grey, rationalist technocratic world. Already throughout Europe, sensitive creative young people are unwilling to submit to the arid conformism and regimentation which much of industry and commerce requires. In Sweden this is now reaching chronic proportions. It is not just a question of monetary reward rather more that young people want space to give vent to their energy, creativity, individuality and emotional and subjective requirements.

So desperate has the situation become that an English senior Technical Manager confided in me "Things are so bad we are really going to have to take seriously the recruitment of women even if that means the odd creche here or there. Say its equal opportunities and the feminists and the socialists will go for it in a big way." But that too seems to be failing as recent reports point out that less women are going into technical computing subjects than in 1985. In the U.S. it is predicted but not only for these reasons that as they enter the 21st century there will be a shortage of some 500,000 engineers and scientists. So what is in train is the imposition of values, ways of behaving, cultural expectations which so diminish our self image and render us so passive and machine dependant that a technocratic rule based world will begin to seem normal and acceptable.

But this approach is not without its deep contradictions and dilemmas. If it is possible to produce this conformist mechanistic fodder for the "real world" there is the related problem that they must not be so conformist as to be totally void of some spark of originality. Otherwise where will the product innovation programmes and new markets come from? On the other hand, too much originality, creativity and imagination would be perceived as systems disturbance and would be unacceptable. So we are back to our material specification – a narrow band of acceptability, not good, not bad but just right. So there are the hosts of psychologists and psychiatrists (not quite as bad as those in the Soviet Union who pleased their Stalinist masters by consigning non conformists to asylums), frantically supporting human resource development specialists in producing computer based interviewing programmes where the right answer is always infinitely preferable to an interesting one. Programmes which ensure that the not too grovelling little conformist is always the winner.

CHAPTER 4

THE ABOLITION OF CHILDHOOD

As with our factory model, the state of the component or "Human operating unit" at this final inspection stage is linked in the development process to the initial raw material state, our childhood. Just as raw material in conventional production has to be monitored, tested and scientifically prepared for its ultimate destination so also must human material be scientifically prepared as society moves towards its factory model. In this regard, childhood in the sense in which I will describe it, is a real problem indeed. It is notoriously unscientific, is unstructured, is supervised by amateurs and non professionals, namely parents, and by definition the activists are the children themselves. For the reductionist bent on scientific principle and engineering precision, this is clearly a recipe for chaos and an unmitigated disaster. Above all, childhood is a subversive hotbed for the spread of tacit knowledge. This is a term coined by Polanyi to describe that form of knowledge which as he put it, is "those things we know but cannot tell".

The reductionists and so called rationalists display a passionate [sic] dislike of this form of knowledge since it cannot be stated explicitly and therefore cannot be reduced to rules. I discussed it once with a leading American Professor who was developing expert systems in the medical field. I discussed the dangers of assuming that the vast range of human knowledge and commitment could be reduced to rules, and suggested instead that what we needed was a rich creative interaction between tacit knowledge and a rule-based core. I suggested that rule based systems could clearly be of help to medical practitioners but that in parallel with this, the tacit dimension of their capability should likewise be expanded, as we are attempting to do in fields of engineering. He counted each point scientifically until I asked him what he thought of Polanyi. "Look Mike", he said earnestly, "Polanyi is a pain in the arse". I immediately divined that this was not a medical diagnosis at all, but rather his primitive way of saying that he didn't like Polanyi. It's a bit like that with childhood. For the reductionists, childhood is just one big pain in the arse.

Childhood, that marvellous developmental, experimental, learning-by-doing progression is for them, unscientific chaos. Very early on the child emits sounds. It cries, and this may be of a niggling form or of distress. A parent, usually a mother, can detect the significance of this. The child gurgles when it is pleased. It does this without knowing the frequency or the amplitude of the signals it is creating but they work, and they work better day by day. Whilst still lying on its back in the pram, the child detects a rattle suspended on an elastic cord stretched across the pram. It learns to pull it and knows that the harder it pulls the further the rattle moves away from the horizontal. This is understood by the child without knowing the theory of the triangular forces. Having pulled the cord downwards, the child releases it and sees that it projects upwards. This also is understood by the child without knowing theories of strain energy in materials. It soon engages in that extraordinary balancing act – standing up. If inclined to topple over one way, the child leans its weight in the other and outstretches its arm to restore balance without knowing about centres of gravity and centres of percussion. Eventually, and to the delight of its parents, it takes its first steps without any instruction in dynamics, advised only by parental encouragement and non-scientific communication such as "Come to Daddy". In those first few weeks of walking, as it waddles around the kitchen, it acquires and displays extraordinary knowledge of three dimensional space. As it moves round objects, occasionally holding on to rigid ones which will have afforded some support, waddling precariously towards the table and crouching down at the last moment to avoid crashing its head by changing the magnitude of its z co-ordinate in three dimensional space.

It is clear however, as it begins to play, that the knowledge absorption is extraordinary. Catching a ball is an extraordinary achievement. At first the child is unable to predict the point at which it should intercept it. Even when the ball is thrown directly to it, it may close its hands an instant too early and miss the ball, or an instant too late and it will bounce off its chest but hand, eye and brain co-ordination develop rapidly through this practice. The eyes will assess the flight path of the ball, will ensure that the child moves to the correct position to intercept it with appropriate acceleration and deceleration, and the hands will close to grasp it with impeccable timing. All this is performed without knowing the theory of trajectories.

Soon other capacities such as tree climbing will develop. Precarious thin branches will be bent as the child moves outwards along its length, testing its maximum bending moment, without knowing about its third moment of area, or having even a passing acquaintance with Timochenko's strength of materials. The odd test to destruction as a branch breaks, serves as a sharp and sometimes painful reminder of the limits of structures, and will be stored in the mind's great memory bank as a typical case to be used for future reference. Social skills and negotiation with peers develop apace without recourse to social theory. If a child won't share its toys or behaves unacceptably, the potential playmate may dramatically exit from the scene in a manner that puts Peggy Lee's rendition of "I don't want to play in your yard, I don't like you any more" to shame.

Over and above all this however, the child is learning the most complicated thing they can ever learn. More complicated than that which they might learn if they ultimately take a Ph.D in pure mathematics or theoretical physics. They are learning natural language. The phenomenon of natural language is so complex that we don't really understand it, yet all human beings are capable of it because it is expected of them because culturally it is required of them, and above all because it is transmitted naturally. We learn it through the dynamic of doing it, usually from our mothers, so we have in most languages terms such as "The Mother Tongue" or "Die Muttersprache". As we start to learn it, nobody tells us "This is a noun, a subordinate adjectival clause or a verb. Indeed if they did so, we would probably never learn to speak. We learn it too, without knowing the theories of Chomsky or that Wittgenstein's words are supposed to define themselves by their use.

This way of knowing, this sense of shape, size and form ill prepares one for a world where everything is supposed to be rule based and predetermined and highley structured and regulated. Not only does it not prepare one for such a world, but the reductionists see it as a dangerous form of cultural opposition. They do not see the rich possibility of this type of knowing being ultimately supported by theory and enhanced by providing computers and systems which support that rich dimension of human capability rather than objectivising it and eliminating it. And so because they can only see it as a reservoir of otherness, an oppositional base with which they cannot cope, they seek to eliminate it, and so it is that childhood is being abolished. There will be no law enacted to bring this about. It will not be written into party manifestos. Like so many of the big issues which confront humanity, it will not be announced at all. After all, nobody announced the destruction of nature. They simply got on with the task in a myriad of small and big ways.

Just about everybody in the technologically advanced nations was involved at one level or another in that process. Only when the destruction became glaringly manifest, were voices raised in opposition at the point at which it is almost too late. Had anybody announced that they were going to destroy nature and eliminate vast ranges of flora and fauna, change climatic conditions, turn cows into cannibals, pollute the rivers and the air, there would have been an uproar. Likewise if it were announced that childhood was going to be abolished, there would also be an uproar. What is so particularly insidious is that no announcement is required because the process is so endemic to our technocratic culture that we are not really aware that we are doing it.

The processes are well in hand. Schooling will start earlier and earlier. Childhood will be highly structured and regimented. That destructive process of exams will start earlier and earlier. Pastimes such as they are, will be increasingly passive. Average television viewing time is now significant. Sports will be highly specialised and systematised. The capacity to make our own toys, entertain ourselves and organise our own play will go and this will be allocated to professionals who will do it on our behalf.

This is unnecessary and undesirable. We all of us know deep down how important unstructured events have been to us in our lifetime, and those unstructured playful events so often lay the basis for our subsequent capacity to be creative, imaginative and involved. My own experiences are perhaps not uncommon of many of my generation. I loved playing with water in small streams. We made small locks with one outlet, and by putting a small boat in the narrowing section, it would accelerate. I gained there a deep sense of hydrodynamics, which years later served me to good effect when I was studying Venturi phenomena.

We had a game where we would take pieces of wood and pass them round and each of us would have to say what it was we saw in the wood. Some saw clenched fists, others the heads of reptiles. For some there were horses with flowing manes and others rugged mountains as the imagination was stimulated and flowed. Years later, I found that this form of pattern recognition and imagination helped in discerning patterns in complex structures of information. Wandering through woods one saw sycamore seeds helicopting with gravity-defying slowness. In storms, the trees moved in majestic motions, which subsequently advised work on aerodynamics in the aerospace industry.

In the summer we were in Galway, there was the fascination of seeing the salmon return and wondering what guidance system it was that enabled them to return to the very point at which they had been spawned. In October, whilst playing in the fields one saw the great skeens of geese majesticly return from foreign lands. There was the speculation how they could possibly do it – were they guided by the stars? Were they following some magnetic lines?

Then there were the story telling games. One would start the story and the next would have to follow on, and each would weave their own thoughts in their own particular way, into the fabric of the zigzagging story. The power of language and expression and imagery was displayed, if only at a primitive level, by games in which one would tell a story to see if one could make the others laugh or far, far more challengingly, who could make up a story which would make the others cry?

Then there were the stories told by adults. There were the old, classical highly stylised stories homed to perfection through generations of embellishment yet each time revealed with new energy, meaning and expression of the individual storyteller. Stories that conveyed figuratively, beautifully and analogically the master ideas of a culture – notions of heroism, of good, of evil, of justice and injustice, of the qualitive and the quantitative. Then there were the made up stories or 'makey-ups' as they were called, where the child would designate a topic about a haunted house, about a dragon, about a child being a bird or being chased by Monzy Kirwin. Some were simply awful, and others were masterpieces of improvisation. In some cases they were negotiable, and the child could intervene and say "This happened" or "Could you let that happen?" It was not that these stories were good or bad but rather that they were alive as the imagination and concentration was exercised and extended.

It wasn't only the story but the way it was told, the intonation, the facial expression of the storyteller and the gestures. That great storytelling tradition is dying out across Europe and with it, part of our heritage and our culture, and it is dying out at a time when new communication technologies, creatively used, could facilitate a renaissance and bring back for millions of children a dimension of childhood – imagination, involvement and sheer excitement which would prepare them to contribute actively and creatively in the reformulation of the future.

Then there were the fairy tales. They were usually read by women, mothers, elder sisters or the inevitable aunts (Nannies?) or better still they were simply told. Those told were always the best. They were more raucous, more ferocious, more frightening (spine chilling?), more descriptive and more committed than the written ones. The told stories were part of a great historical, oral tradition. It was a matriarchal tradition which transmitted imagery, wisdom and human emotions in a way that was at once theatrical, descriptive, delightful, humanistic and horrifying. So long as it was oral, informal and for small groups, it was safe. Once it began to be written, it had to be well structured and sanitised. The Brothers Grimm have much to answer for as well as to be thanked for.

The stories were long and complex. They were convoluted and analogical. They required and received wrapped attention. They were a hopeless preparation for the frenzied instant gratification of the 2.4 minute mind of the American T.V. zapper. The story unfolded slowly and graphically. Powerful images had to be constructed and internalised if the story was to be savoured and garnished to its glorious culmination. It stimulated, stretched and fed the imagination. Only the aridness of our reductionist minds and the delinquent genius of our species could insult them by saying they are only fairy tales, but above all, they are true. Part of our world is populated by monsters and giants and poisoned dwarfs. Only fairy tales could prepare us for that distorted dwarf Adolf Hitler. What analytical historian would have predicted the coming of such a monster? What novelist would have had the audacity to construct a tale in which an unknown, uneducated Austrian down-and-out could seize the mind of the great nation that produced Beethoven and Goethe, Schiller and Leibniz? What science fiction writer would have the audacity to portray this bizarre figure driving millions of solid citizens into murderous hysteria with his verbal orgasms? Then there was his manic, dialectical twin Stalin, the mass murderer of millions, indeed tens of millions of his own people. The Romanians know that there are monsters who creep out from their palaces and destroy complete villages and round up the locals to imprison them in engines known as High Rise Flats. There are real Pol Pot-type creatures who creep out from the undergrowth to transform the pathways of life into the killing fields of death.

There are the evil gnomes who can so distract mothers in Third World countries that they feed their children strange potions rather than their own milk of life, and ensure an infant mortality rate 10 times higher than would otherwise be the case. There are those whose powers are so awesome that they have turned mother nature into a junky, incapable of producing without her next chemical fix. That which children keep at the cautionary imagery of our conciousness is transformed into nauseating reality day in, day out by the delinquent genius of our species.

Hansel and Gretel are all around us, abandoned in the forests of the inner cities. They roam confused through the corridors of social services departments and in and out of the filing cabinets of caring agencies. In a society which can't see the woods for the trees, they wander dazed through the thickets and undergrowth; through court orders, orphanages and local council care centres. But children do know in a Lurie-like – Alison Lurie, author of *Don't tell the grown ups* – fashion from the deep collective consciousness of our species, that Jack can kill the giant and steal his treasure, that monsters and evil queens do get their comeuppances and they suspect that there was a parallel story, *The Sleeping Prince*, who was rescued from enchantment by an active heroin. They sense too that ordinary people can be enterprising and energetic and bold and persistent and that's not just a plot on the part of their rulers to keep them happily in their place. Above all they probably sense that if we are to have artists, writers, poets, singers, creative caring inventors, those who can make the blind see, the deaf hear and the lame walk, then we do need people who can weave spells, sing so beautifully that it drives away the spirits of depression, climb glass mountains, outwit evil spirits, confound stupid brutal rulers, buck authority and create magic objects. Above all to see, as in a fairy tale, the good and the evil, the beauties and the horrors, the dungeons and the palaces and always to hold that childlike optimism which encourages us to seek the healing potion that will break the blinding spell and allow us to see the beauty and the magic that is life and nature itself.

It is rather that it has a life of its own which arises out of the inner logic of the unquestioned and unquestionable, namely progress.

CHAPTER 5

EICHMANN IN THE MAKING

I have shown above, that within the production model, the nature of the required end-product determines the processing of the raw materials from the very onset. So it is with educational production.

That which they call education is not in fact education at all, but compliance training, the end product being what commerce and industry requires. It is true also of all major bureacracies such as government departments and the product is what I call occupational Eichmen. Like Eichmann, they will do what they are told, and their defence whenever challenged, is that they were simply following the rules. In their corporate roles, they produce equipment which pollutes the environment; they instigate, then directly and indirectly support policies which result in the destruction of the rain forests. You can find them running development corporations which destroy the centres of cities and communities. As engineers they design systems of a Chernobyl and Sellafield kind and work in companies and bureacracies that spend billions on armaments production.

In their corporate role the industrial Eichmen are happy to do all this without questioning the multiplier effects of their work. Furthermore, they succeed in isolating themselves from economic realities worldwide. They become everyday models of Dr Jekyll and Mr Hyde, since the educational system can't of course completely succeed in destroying all aspects of their sensitivity and humanity. What it does do is show them that these concerns must take place outside their work, and so we get a further division between the human being as a producer and as a consumer, between the so-called real world (by which is meant the commercial bureaucratic world) and the unreal world, which is the personal and the community.

A kind of schizophrenia is developed in which these industrial Eichmen in their corporate role, will pollute the environment, clog up centres of cities, close factories and sack thousands of people. When home, they will take their children on their knees and, on occasion, collect for their local jumble sale in aid of the village hall. At home they can be human and civilised but at work they are the rabid technologists, the tooth and claw Attilas of development war. Even the Church of England has now raised the moral and ethical questions associated with this split personality.

The split is of course, instigated very early on. In the plot to destroy childhood, schooling (not at all to be confused with education) will start earlier and earlier. From an early stage, children are conditioned to accept the notorious proposition that you learn at school and university from teachers, but that you are not learning when you are at home with your parents, neither when you are with your friends nor when you are playing games: that you are not learning from your trade union activity or from involvement with your local community group mobilising against the motorway about to be put in your backgarden.

One is frequently asked if schools are really successful. The answer must be that they are incredibly successful in producing the kind of people required by the vast multinationals and bureaucracies. The disastrous state the world is in, and the minimalist reaction we seek to the absurdities about us, is eloquent tribute to the educational system. Brecht once pointed out how successful school is at producing the kind of people society requires. He recalled that on his first day at school, all the children were required to stand round the hall. The teacher then shouted that they should get a desk. They rushed for the desks, and some were left without one. The teacher whacked them, and when Brecht complained that there were no desks left, the teacher said "That is the first lesson you have got to learn. There are always too few desks."

My dislike of school arises directly from my love of education and learning. Yet we have been conditioned to believe the opposite. As Illich points out:

> "School is an institution built on the axiom that learning is the result of teaching and institutional wisdom continues to accept this axiom despite overwhelming evidence to the contrary. We have all learned most of what we know outside school. Pupils do most of their learning without, and often despite their teachers. Most tragically, the majority of men are taught their lessons by schools even though they never go to school. Everybody learns how to live outside school. We learn to speak, to think, to love, to feel, to play, to curse, to politic and to work without the interference of a teacher."

Furthermore, modern education tends to stimulate the delinquent in our species rather than support the genius of our humanity.

The school is a very recent phenomenon. It has only been around for about 200 years and coincides with the growth of industrial society and the production model of society as a whole. If we succeed in getting through the next few decades without destroying ourselves and the environment, we may overcome our delinquency just as we shall have to abandon the productionist model of society, so too we will abandon the school as a destructive historical aberration.

Meantime, the school holds sway, and most people in industrial society do take schools seriously. Their acceptance is based on a number of myths: they profess to be providing education, when in fact they increasingly provide arid ritualistic training. They claim legitimacy as descendents of the great medieval schools of learning when in fact, they are the very antithesis of these.

The medieval schools of learning provided for the transmission of a culture acquired through major projects. The projects may have been the building of a church, the decoration of a monastery and so on. The culture was transmitted by working alongside a master who was a "doer" as distinct from a teacher in the modern sense. That system provided for a much more holistic development than is possible in our present day fragmented society. It produced the Giottos, Leonardos, and Brunelleschis whose range of competence subsumed painting, sculpture, machine design, engineering ... Their abilities are the more astonishing given the lack of resources, support systems and equipment.

The products of our educational systems of today are pygmies by comparison. We still define our civilisation by the art forms, structures, artefacts and illustrated manuals produced by the great schools of learning. They involved handling wide bands of uncertainty, uncertainty of materials, of construction techniques, and of experimentation with new materials. Above all, the knowledge they developed was tacit knowledge which linked hand and brain in a meaningful productive process.

In contrast, schools today in their factory-like mode are obsessed with certainty. You read a certain book in a certain manner, undertake certain exercises in a predetermined way.

You answer examination-type questions in a given form and you are successful. The school radiates the value system of the technocratic, scientific society obsessed as it is with predictability, repeatability and quantifiability. Like the factory, it is highly structured. So highly structured that what goes on there, although it masquerades as education, is in fact arid training.

Training provides for narrow machine or systems-specific competences, precisely in accordance with the factory model. Not too much nor too little is provided, but just enough for the immediate task in hand.

My hierarchy of verbs is that one programmes a robot, one trains a dog or possibly a soldier and one provides educational developmental environments for human beings. Our schools are really quite competent at producing the soldiers for industrial society.

Education is an altogether different matter. It is in many ways, a state of mind embodied within a culture. Instead of programmed learning, it encourages creativity and excitement about new ideas, the imaginative exploration of issues, critical capabilities and a love of the exchange of ideas.

Schools on the other hand, carefully follow the factory model. There are different rooms to simulate different workshops for different processes. Each process is fragmented and separated from the other, and just as in industry there are quality control procedures, in the schools are the examinations.

Examinations are based on a defect model. They are better at exposing what we don't know rather than what we do know. For example, the system is incapable of distinguishing between a 'good' student or a 'bad' student unless one or other of them make some "mistakes". There are right answers and wrong answers and it is quickly conveyed that interesting answers don't count. Rather than enjoy or be interested in subjects, pupils learn to answer examination-type questions about them. Books are not read for enjoyment, they're scavenged for facts and standardised forms of analysis examine them out of existence. The whole system is geared to a final binary decision of pass/not pass, rather than providing interests, commitments and motivations which will facilitate a many faceted development.

School conveys the idea that narrow factual information is more important than contextual understanding and commitment, that bureaucratic, administrative, rational, logical knowledge is more important than tacit and manual skill. Above all, it is good at finding out who displays the particular flaws and stumbles at the particular pitfalls where the traps have been set. The school's ultimate aim is a quality control procedure which allows the component to move to the next stage of production integration called the university. It is a process which produces, for its own internalised requirements, a different form of human being, the 'schoolchild' (not to be confused with childhood), and the 'senior pupil' (not to be confused with adolescence).

This special species of human being is for the major part separated from the rest of society and its activities. It is a segregation based on age. This damaging process means that children are separated from adults at work. The liberal minded see this as good as they are still smarting from what happened to children during the industrial revolution, but the industrial revolution, which in Britain put children in the mines and was a mere fraction (though an awful fraction) of time, should not be confused with the totality of human existence.

Children in agricultural communities undertaking small, simple tasks alongside their parents learned to be useful whilst at the same time enjoying childhood. Playfulness was linked as it always should be, with social and useful activities. A subtle sense of how things are done and organised was conveyed in an unstructured way simply "by being there". This tradition has not yet been entirely destroyed. Whilst recently making the film about Brunelleschi in Italy, I watched the construction of a beautiful hand cut glass partition. It was clearly a three generation family working on it. The youngest was but 6 or 7, possibly not yet at school. The father was at the top, fixing the glass sections into a frame which the grandfather held in position. They were using specially produced bronze screws of different type and size. The father would throw one down to the child to indicate the type he required. The child would explore with excitement, the range of drawers to select some of a similar length and diameter. These he would hand to the grandfather who in turn would present them up for fixing in position. The child was learning so much by being involved in these activities and by listening to the verbal exchanges between the adults. He was gaining a sense of confidence in the realisation that if his father and grandfather could produce beautiful structures of this kind, so could he. It was subtly imbuing a sense of quality and craftsmanship, and above all a sense of competence.

Likewise, in some of the ethnic minority communities in the United Kingdom, quite young children help their parents in their small family businesses and shops.

Let me make it clear that I am not here talking about child labour or the exploitation of young people. I am talking about participation in activities. In one such shop which I sometimes visit in the West London area, a nine year old

Indian girl glows with excitement in finding the product that one has requested and this in an astonishing mixture of products in a small store. She knows the price of all of them, is capable of giving change, and if the specific product requested is not available can even sometimes, emerge from the array of shelves with a proposed alternative. We lose much when we separate children from that kind of involvement.

In this case, the process of learning is a gradual 'learning by doing' one, with continuous feedback and in contact with a real learning situation rather than an assimilated one. What a contrast it poses to the ritualistic pressure of examinations which converges on a frenzied binary choice with enormous pressure on young people, pressure to such an extent that in Japan sadly and now in Ireland, some young people commit suicide because of the benign tyranny of a system which conveys to them that if they do not succeed at that point, they are lost forever!

The obsession with examinations is now horrific in – strangely enough – Ireland. Radio programmes describe the leaving certificate examination papers each day. Serious newspapers such as the *Irish Times* have assessments of the quality and nature of the questions and everything is focused on a sort of educational Darwinism where members of the whole community – in particular the parents – are onlookers in this awful 'go/no go' situation. When the results are out the papers publish a points race scale advising on the course one can pursue with a given number of exam points. For example, someone who had a burning desire to be a physicist may end up reading medicine or architecture because that is the only option their points will allow.

It is not possible or desirable to revert to forms of educational development which applied in the great schools of learning. It is however, desirable to look at the aspects of those schools which might be applicable to the problems of our modern society and at the same time provide for more holistic forms of education. One distinct possibility would be forms of project learning; that is to say the school in a new and reconstructed form, will select and work on a series of projects. These should relate to local issues which nonetheless embody more universal principles. In Germany for example, some schools are adopting a local river or stream. In the physics class they produce small instruments which will measure the velocity of flow. In the chemistry class they work out ways of measuring the levels of pollution and analyse the chemical composition of the water. In the biology class they take samples from the river to assess the development of wildlife there. In the art classes they make drawings of particular parts of the river or the activities which take place upon it. In the economics classes they assess the economic significance of the river and these are then related to more broadly based issues of pollution worldwide, economic matters, acid rain and so on. Compositions on the river are written in the language classes and in one case where pollution killed some of the fish, quite moving poetry was written by the children about the impact of pollution on this environment.

Some projects are related to demographic changes in some German cities. Given the growing number of the population over 65, projects investigate the role older people could play and how they can be involved in transmitting accounts of the past to younger generations; what their physical and medical requirements are and what kind of involvement they could have within their communities.

Other projects include designing pieces of equipment for the elderly and studies with the elderly in analysing the sort of buildings and equipment they require. Thus overall, there is a heightened awareness of social and community issues. Also, as a result of interactions with the elderly people, an understanding is developed across generations and simple and direct means of communication are evolved within practice.

Other forms of projects have involved establishing a daily school newspaper. Methods have to be developed for assessing news items, for restucturing the news in forms which make them appropriate to the school and its pupils and relating major news items to local issues, such as the likely impact of new policies within the EEC. Many projects relate to issues of energy conservation. A school in Britain is developing a low energy city car in conjunction with local polytechnics and local industry. In other words, the project becomes a focal point and stimulus for a broad-based and holistic form of educational development, which facilitates the integration of different subject areas and provides a means for continuous assessment and an ultimate test of how the project functions in practice. This is more desirable than the negative destructiveness of conventional examination procedures.

It also means that the 16 and 17 year olds working on the project have to learn how best to communicate with these external experts, how to acquire knowledge from them and how to organise their abilities at appropriate stages in the project. This would lay the basis for the continuation at university level, of the kind of project based degrees which are now being introduced on an experimental basis in Germany and in Britain. I have been acquainted with one of these project based degrees. Following six months general education, the student or group of students selected a major project. It involved designing and building a prototype of a new form of city car. In the early stages, assessments had to be made of what kinds of transport systems will be acceptable in future in cities. It was necessary to consider the long term environmental impacts of transport systems.

Once a design specification had been agreed, the actual technical work on the project commenced. They were going to use a permanent magnet motor so it was necessary for them to select an appropriate member of staff in this field who would work for them on the project. This constituted a role reversal where the lecturer was a resource and was 'used' by the students. They had to plan how to make best use of that person's time and integrate that expert's time with a range of other experts who were giving them advice on the design of the transmission system, the suspension, the steering and the body. They were acquiring knowledge in the way they might have done in medieval times when an apprentice or 'improver' was working with a master craftsman. They learned to apply mathematical formulae to real world problems. Since they were building real prototypes, they had to acquire workshop technology skills.

The first students to graduate from these courses are extremely competent people, for this form of learning activity produces proactive, self conscious young people rather than ones who passively respond to a factory-like system.

The enthusiasm these types of project elicit accords with my own experience. I was fortunate enough when I was about 16 to encounter a gifted craftsman, Sean Cleary, who happened also to be working as the craft metalwork teacher in our school. He had worked with companies in England and elsewhere in Europe, and could bring a wide range of practical experience to the task involved. Above all, he transmitted a sense of excitement about discovery, design and good quality engineering craftsmanship. He had a superb sense of materials and the means by which they could be formed, machined and surface finished. I still remember the excitement I felt when looking at the rings of light on the surfaces of slip gauges which he had lapped.

As part of a project which was really extra curricular, we agreed to design and build a double acting steam engine. The workshop facilities available were very limited indeed and in fact constituted only a lathe and a drilling machine. We did not even have a milling machine. As a result, ingenuity had to substitute for fixed capital. Ingenious devices were prepared such that we could mill on the lathe. We devised means by which we could index upon it and since we had no means of forging the crankshaft, we actually fabricated one with precision finished pieces which were assembled with push-fit tolerances and dowelled joints. In that remote area of the West of Ireland in the early 50's, there was a chronic lack of appropriate engineering materials. We were confronted with great problems when it came to finding appropriate close-grained cast iron for some of the components.

Had the schooling been conventional, one would have written an extensive report describing the kinds of materials required, then setting out the problems of attempting to locate them and finally explaining in detail why the project was not possible due to the lack of appropriate facilities and materials. The end result would have been a report not a product. Had that been the form of education, no doubt one would have ended up as a first class bureaucrat. Probably, a senior post in the Civil Service would be in prospect.

The project however was based on a deep intentionality and motivation. The intention was to make a double acting steam engine that really would function. Driven by that kind of motivation, a creative search was made in all kinds of areas for appropriate cast iron. Eventually, rumour had it that in an old disused sawmill there existed a large flywheel. It followed that the material in a flywheel, because of its centrifugal stresses would have been material of reasonable quality. I still recall setting out some 40 years ago with my mentor, friend and teacher Sean Cleary to track down the elusive sawmill and the even more elusive flywheel. We set out equipped with a hacksaw and some half a dozen blades, aware that this was going to be a fairly arduous manual task. I recall the hours we spent in cutting out a major piece from the flywheel, and how working on the material in that way, one was aware of the texture of the material and the best ways of cutting it to get a section most appropriate to our requirements.

When eventually we liberated the piece we required from the rim of the flywheel, the relationship of weight to total volume was very clear indeed, particularly as this had to be transported on a bicycle some six miles back to the school. In a modest childlike way, one was reminded of Leonardo's lovely description of his visits to the quarries to retrieve large pieces of marble for use in statues they were producing. Simple drawings had to be made of all the components, tolerances were based on experience of the thermal expansion of the materials. Appropriate materials had to be selected to act as bearings and slideways, so that they would "not bind".

That steam engine is to this day one of my prized possessions and I learned more in that project than many of the much more formalised "lessons".

I attempt to show elsewhere in this book, that when we achieve something, however modest or however complex, our culture conditions us to believe that it has been the outcome of a highly structured and formalised way of proceeding. In point of fact, this is seldom the case. Accidental occurrences, unplanned encounters, capacities to recognise an opportunity, brainwaves, flashes of inspiration, passing stimulus remarks by colleagues, an inexplicable interest in a subject and a motivation are the real and unstructured ways in which we proceed through life. However, our culture requires us to deny this and so we construct a rationalist explanation for the manner in which we proceed and feel compelled to make it look logical and scientific at every point. When we free ourselves from the constraints of this reductionism, we realise that it was the unstructured events in our lives from which we learned most and which guide the way we proceed in a whole complex of developing situations.

Likewise, when we look back on our schooling, we at first believe it was the highly structured, organised parts of that process that mattered. Then, on deeper reflection we know that that was not so. In my own case, it was the unstructured and in many cases, out-of-school activities that had the greatest effect upon my subsequent career development.

School of course serves other purposes than that of preparing the units of production for industrial society. It legitimises the notion that there has to be some who are winners, some who are losers and that the winners are a tiny minority with the majority being losers. The system convinces the losers that it is their own fault, that they are simply (to use the school term) not up to the grade. This destruction of expectation takes place in British schools as early as the 11 plus (still operating in some areas). The school functions like a sort of distillation column, pouring out its products at different levels. It conditions people to accept their place in society and socialises and legitimises inequalities in all their manifest forms. Most tragically, it constitutes a disastrous wastage of talent. It conditions us to think of people as competent and incompetent, as skilled and unskilled when we should think of our fellow human beings and ourselves as always reservoirs of potential with an extraordinary capacity to absorb new ideas, to develop new talents and above all, to be interested and involved.

School destroys much of that. It maims people, and then blames them for their resultant disability. As with production, it assumes a one best way for the next level of processing. This is the University. Gradually the University comes to be assumed as the only way forward, rather than just yet another way that might be helpful. Professional forms of development in which people learn by doing are gradually closed off. Previously people could qualify as accountants, solicitors, engineers, architects and bankers by working alongside the professionals either as apprentices or articled clerks.

Denmark still retains a professional route to engineering qualifications and Germany has retained the second and third routes to qualifications. It is still not unusual in German Universities to meet professors of engineering who will proudly proclaim in their CV's that they were apprentices at Mercedes or elsewhere. An apprenticeship-type training in Britain or the United States is now a sort of indelible mark which will prevent further progress since the quality control procedures determine that only those who have failed at school proceed to apprenticeships. In consequence, well tried routes of education and learning, forms which produced the giants of the Industrial Revolution like Brunel and Maudslay are now rapidly closing off worldwide.

This is true not only in engineering and scientific pursuits but also in the arts. We may reflect on the fact that Bach,

Mozart and Beethoven did not go to school in the form we now know it, nor did they go to University in current terms. Yet in spite of highly structured teaching processes, including A Levels in music and rigorous entrance requirements to music faculties, it can hardly be claimed that we are producing people who compare even remotely with those mentioned above. Likewise, I would question whether our architects are as competent and imaginative as those produced historically by the master/apprentice relationship.

So we move towards a 'certified society' which operates a form of certification of exclusion rather than one of inclusion. At all levels, people are being intimidated into believing that they cannot sing unless they have been to music college, cannot act unless they have been to drama school, cannot paint unless they have been to art college so the idea of a culture which expects and allows that people can only participate meaningfully in these activities if they are dedicated professionals is thus established.

Even those certified will not venture far out of their own narrow, arid terrain. Given today's educational and certification outlook, it seems inconceivable that Brunelleschi, who served a seven year apprenticeship as a goldsmith, could ultimately have designed and built the largest and most complex dome in Christendom. Or, to take a more recent example, that Brunel, who served an apprenticeship as an instrument maker, could design the massive and complex structures which still grace London's major stations. Brunel could probably not get even a minor post as a structural engineer or an architect in a local government department today because he hadn't been to university.

Recruitment procedures reinforce these developments. Computer based systems and interactive computer interviewing techniques have rigidly prescribed criteria. At the first level, the applicant must be "a graduate". Those who are not are excluded. Promotion procedures within companies likewise deny the development of those who simply have the interest and capacities to progress. These procedures of exclusion apply equally in left wing and right wing-type structures. Indeed in many ways, in their notion of so-called progress, left wing organisations are the worst. Right wing ones will often be opportunist enough to recognise a self starter. Left wing local authorities massively discriminate against those whose experience of the world is real and practical. In my experience, their notion of upgrading some jobs was to declare that they required graduate qualification for them. The outcome was that those already doing the work competently were no longer allowed to undertake it and graduates (in however an irrelevant or disconnected subject) would be selected, frequently becoming the laughing stock of those around them. Large numbers of competent people abandoned local authority work and simply became self employed, where they would experience some dignity.

In building restoration programmes instigated by left wing authorities, the bureaucrats would not allow craftsmen to have apprentices working with them, because these craftsmen were not "qualified instructors". The fact that they had been successfully transmitting their knowledge to a future generation over a period of 20 or 30 years, did not count in this rigid system of certification. And so there was (and is still), a waste of talent on every level and a resentment by those who have competences that they are (like the craftsmen) prevented from transmitting them to future generations.

CHAPTER 6

COGS TYRANNIC

"I turn my eyes to the schools and universities of Europe and
there behold the loom of Locke, whose woof rages dire, washed
by the waterwheels of Newton. Black the cloth in heavy wreaths
folds over every nation. Cruel works of many wheels I view,
wheel without wheel with cogs tyrannic..."

William Blake, *Man and Work*

What then is the shape, form and objective of this processing
plant the university, for which the young have been
instructed, tested, rejected, accepted, formed and structured
for the first 18 years of their lives? We may firstly observe
that it is a processing plant which confers a quality control
tag on its product enabling it to be an acceptable component
in that final assembley which we know as society.

In spite of its vigorous claims to the contrary, the
university is concerned with standardisation and
interchangeability of its products. Whilst there are good
universities and bad universities the assumption is that a
graduate in (let us say) physics or engineering from any
university any place in the world is broadly interchangeable
with a graduate from the other side of the universe. They
contribute to a globalisation of standardisation in the way
production systems do. A component made for a Ford
vehicle in the United States should be interchangeable with
one made in Germany for a similar model. The principles of
engineering taught to an undergraduate in China will more

and more be similar to that taught to an undergraduate in Britain or in Germany.

The one best way, the optimum set of subjects and topics and ways of teaching them is gradually being synthesised and engineering techniques involving different materials – say bamboo structures (with each member having its own closed compartments which at one stage inspired the notion of barquettes in our ships) will gradually be eliminated. Techniques which accord with local aesthetic concerns, cultural or religious traditions or practices, even geographical considerations would be ruthlessly levelled down to the one best way.

Within production we talk about "Families of parts" and these characterisations are internationally applicable. Likewise the graduate in one country will have far more in common with a graduate of a similar subject in another country than with compatriots of their own country or even members of their own family or village. The graduate from an underdeveloped third world country will think more in terms of European and American engineering solutions than those which are more appropriate to his/her domestic situation. They will learn to conform at all levels speaking in terms, using expressions peculiar to their subject area rather than that which reflects their own cultural and enviromental background.

National differences do of course exist as between say production engineering as taught in the United States and as taught in West Germany. What we are discussing here is the tendency to compress everything into the conformity of the one best way. The notion that Universities provide the basis and stimulus for the exchange of ideas will become less and less tenable as more and more clone-like figures are produced and where an exchange of ideas will in fact be merely a change of location.

Within production, there are standard communication protocols so that factories can communicate worldwide. The protocol for universities will be a sort of technocratic, proscriptive English. Good car design will be supposed to mean exactly the same in Milan, Cologne, Detroit, Tokyo and all those other countries which aspire to the dubious distinction of producing throw-away cars. In architectural faculties, optimised computer based CAAD (computer aided architectural design) packages will imply that a community design package or an office building expressed in this stylised English will mean, and increasingly does mean, the same in Tokyo, London, New York or Stockholm. Each seeks to create a standardised internal atmosphere, the only minor concession to diversity being the energy input necessary to reflect the reality of external temperature, although that accidental prowess of our global warning may even warm this, as Winter and Summer become less discernible.

In faculties of medicine, expert systems will ensure that diagnostic procedures are standardised worldwide in spite of the growing public interest in alternative forms of medicine.

Over and above these considerations, the universities are increasingly the production units for industrial fodder for the military/industrial complex and its large corporations. The uninhibited quest for truth becomes the uninhibited quest for grants and funding for postgraduate studies so research will be determined by the funds made available from the military/industrial complex. As with the earlier Ford cars you can have any colour so long as it is black and indeed, you can engage in any kind of research so long as the outcome is one required by the large corporations.

Universities are of course not as highly structured as schools. There are still vestiges of concern and even protests. There was the student at Narita airport in Japan, Tiananmen Square in China, and Bucharest in Romania, but an overall ethos exists where such questioning and challenges are seen merely in the industrial context of non compliance and a slight ripple on the curve that is inevitable technological progress.

In the model of the University as a factory, the professors and lecturers are known as operators. Operators in industry perform narrow dedicated tasks in the rarified enviroment of a manufacturing subset. Because they have been narrowly prescribed for their tasks, those in production are often incapable of undertaking any activity in that rarified overdedicated environment. So it is with many academics. They appear competent and they are competent within the very narrow constraints of their tiny self-consistent environment. Outside that, they are frequently lost, literally like fish out of water. They flap and flounder around. Their very isolation and separation from the real world leaves them often singularly incompetent outside their own highly structured little sub-world. I know colleagues well who lecture in economics and finance and whose own domestic economies are a monument to chaos and incompetence.

I know lecturers in social administration who find no difficulty in telling parents and social workers how children should be brought up whilst their relationship with their own children would be a good example of the antithesis of their academic posturing.

I know of lecturers in industrial relations who hold profound courses and run ranges of graduate studies in the nature of industrial relations, democratisation of organisations, power relationships within industry and yet when the governing body of their polytechnic decided to decimate the industrial relations department they were unable to do anything about it. In fact they lacked even the basic competence that a shop steward might display in protecting their jobs and as one governer put it: "It's like putting a knife through butter". The overspecialisation is resulting in what the German students in the 1960s used to call "*Fachidioten*".

Just as overspecialisation in manufacturing itself is now beginning to be counterproductive, so also is it in the Universities. Since the courses must conform more and more to the requirements of scientific criteria, the excitement and passion of the subjects are replaced by arid quantification. In engineering, many courses have now degenerated into a sort of applied mathematics so one ends up with a graduate who is neither a good engineer nor a good physicist. The excitement of engineering discovery, of innovation and construction is gradually lost.

In language departments, the excitement, resonance, turn of phrase of language is replaced by highly formalised, structured and grammatical forms of instruction. One should never ever underestimate the extraordinary ability of academics to turn an exciting, vibrant topic into an incredibly boring routine. In the hope of improving things slightly, some students at British and German universities now present an annual award to the lecturer who delivers the most outstandingly boring lecture. However, far from being reformed by such a demeaning accolade, some lecturers take a perverse pride in winning it and appear to believe, that it shows once again that students really don't know what's good for them.

We may reflect how seldom it is that we encounter say a lecturer of English who is capable of speaking in an exciting and lucid and interesting fashion. We have come to expect something that is grammatical, turgid and lifeless and by God that is what we usually get!

It is vitally important that the growing numbers of mature students are aware of this situation. Women, who will perhaps have brought up a family, had to organise their complex domestic economy on a meagre income, had to plan the procurement of resources and undergo the subtle communications and negotiations involved in bringing up a family, will find that this great knowledge and experience counts virtually for nothing when at a later stage they wish to enter university. The factory-like model does not provide credit for the unstructured learning and tacit knowledge they will have acquired. Lecturers can only really interact with them if they succeed in reducing them to a teacher/pupil relationship where instruction replaces rich interaction and mutual learning and the academic is in control in the unrealistic narrow and constrained environment of their subject area. It would in most cases be better if the courses were to be based on some kind of mutual education where each could learn from the other.

Many young people and also potential mature students question the value of having anything to do at all with universities in their present form.

Business leaders would not necessarily be my role model of what society should be like. However, universities – in particular the business schools – would have us believe that that is where they are created. Many world famous business leaders such as Richard Branson, Alan Sugar, James Goldsmith never attended university and on occasion imply that their ability to cope imaginatively and vigorously with chaotic situations is precisely because they were spared the numbing effect of factory-like conditioning in a university.

This seems to apply also across different cultures. Soichiro Honda set up his piston ring manufacturing business in 1937. He decided he would like to gain some insight into some of the theoretical aspects and arranged to attend night school. He robustly refused to have anything to do with examinations and was therefore refused a qualification. His corporation subsequently developed engines that dominated Formula 1 racing and his cars became best selling models in the United States. He was showered with honorary degrees and doctorates from universities around the world. This is of course true not just in respect of commerce and engineering. One could fill an encyclopaedia with the names of those artists, poets, architects, sculptors, inventors, archeologists and 'people of letters' whose success depended not on university training but rather on motivation, commitment, interest and sheer zest for life. When the Carnegie Foundation for the Advancement of Art sought out Lewis Mumford to examine and report upon the various schools of art throughout the United States, he declined pointing out: "My lack of a degree has become a valuable distinction in America. The PhD is such an inevitable sign of mediocrity here."

Mumford also pointed out that many of the great innovators in the arts, in politics and in the sciences in Victorian times had likewise not attended university.

"I do not wish to be misunderstood here. I am not at all suggesting that universities are irrelevant. They are ideally suited to the way some people wish to develop and learn. What is quite unacceptable is the asumption that this is the one and only way to develop and that those who do not pursue that route are therefore to be seen as some kind of failure. Given the factory nature of this type of education, they may well display characteristics of energy, commitment and sheer excitement which render their way of learning equally valuable, perhaps more valuable in the long term. Above all what I am suggesting is that the university should be seen as merely one way of learning and that at the moment, it is the way which is increasingly suspect and that the university is ripe for radical reform."

But it is unlikely, as Ivan Illich would have it "Only a generation which grows up without obligatory schools will be able to re-create the university" (*Deschooling Society* Page 44). However, just as we could change the factory by introducing Human Centred Systems, so also we could modify the university by introducing student centred project based forms of learning.

Exciting examples, if only in embryo, are already emerging. The North East London Polytechnic in London, has a School of Independent Study. Within the school, it is possible to obtain a degree which is centred on a project which may have been the lifelong concern of a student (who is usually a mature student).

Throughout their lives, they will have developed an interest in a particular subject area: it may be an aspect of architecture or a particular form of engineering, say. I know of ones in the field of nutrition and even learning processes. The mature student will propose a project, will then find members of staff who the student feels have the ability to interact creatively and act as appropriate resources for the development of the project. The project is the focal point around which a variety of subjects are introduced. It is a dynamic, exciting and fulfilling way of studying. It is enriching both to the "student" and the academics involved. It is an open form of learning in which the university or polytechnic is perceived as a resource. Frequently, the projects relate to community concerns, and thus the student can bring a wealth of experience to bear on the topic.

People come with topics which have long excited their imagination. They will have often read in an unstructured way about the topic and will belong to societies or groups who have an interest in that topic. The degree by independent study helps to locate that concern in a wider historical, cultural and educational context. Those working in industry who perhaps witnessed the decline of their sector may wish to analyse alternative forms, so that they and their colleagues might lay the basis for future meaningful employment. Likewise, they bring real human issues and problems to bear as the focal point of such a project. Such learning can now be linked with distributed learning facilties, and new technology can assist in this process. However, as within the Human Centred Model of production, the educational technology must always be merely a tool which the active, engaged, concerned student uses, rather than be a rigid machine to which he or she must slavishly conform.

This is not however, what the 'plant managers' of the future universities are specifying. These universities will not be places where Marcuse-type philosophers will discuss with us the irrationality of our own rationality as we transform ourselves into one dimensional men. They will not, according to this new image, be places where Howard Rosenbrock, in developing his multivariable techniques, will tell us the beautiful cautionary tale of the Lushai Hills Effect.

So that we don't have to overstrain our powers of prediction, those already at the helm of the educational *Titanic* give us a nice succinct definition. "The great university of the future will be that with the great computer system" says Richard Kisett, president of Carnegie Mellon University.

For those who don't like academic one-liners, there is the added explanation for Kisett predicts that his university's computer network will have the same role in student learning, that the development of the assembly line in the 20's had for the production of automobiles: "The assembly line enabled large scale manufacturing to develop. Likewise, the network personal computer system will enable students to increase significantly the amount of learning they do in the university" (both quotes from Roczak in *The Cult of Information* pages 77 & 81).

Let me repeat, I have no objection to computers as tools (in the Heidegger sense) but I do believe education involves much more than interaction with computers. It has to do with face-to-face discussions, reacting to, assimilating and assessing the views of tutors and colleagues, developing critical capacities, being excited about topics.

The extraordinary thing is that these academics who have massive computing power to support their decision making routines and have vast databases which they can draw upon, often fail nonetheless to see the obvious. The obvious is that if they seek to reduce what they do to rules amenable to computer processing in order to ensure that the work they undertake is 'scientific' (in the narrow sense that it implies predictability, repeatability and quantifiability), then they are indeed creating the means of their own destruction.

Medical practitioners who like to pretend that what they do is entirely scientific and devoid of tacit and experiential knowledge and can therefore be embodied in expert systems, find themselves being told that in certain areas of diagnosis the computers are better than they are. This may be true in narrow domains but quite untrue in repsect of holistic medicine.

Likewise, if academics seek to reduce the university to a factory model where learning is rule based, where they seek to make human imagination quantifiable, where they believe that the range of human competences is predictable and narrowly verifiable, then they are reducing themselves to machine-like behaviour. One thing they will forget at their peril, human beings are very bad and incompetent as machines. If we reduce ourselves to the level of machines and try to compete with them, machines in their narrow sense will always be better than we are.

And so the delinquent genius of our species, having sought to rationalise everything, to ignore that which is subjective and non-quantifiable, has driven us to the state where we are, in growing numbers, frantically assembling the psychological and the technological means of our own decline.

CHAPTER 7

THE ONE BEST WAY

I have been attempting to show that the forms of science and technology that we have developed, now constitute a major impediment to the further development of civilisation. Techniques, practices and procedures which at one stage of our development may have been appropriate may now be counter productive in our linear drive forward. The lateral rather than the linear development of our technologies is more appropriate. The fact that at one historical stage it was appropriate in an evolutionary sense that the strongest of the tribe should climb to the nearest hill to see what was on the other side, should not mean that with the awesome power technology has given us, we should continue in a sort of tribal drive for conquest of everything in sight.

One of the most dangerous aspects of all of this lies at the very root of our science and technology itself. That is the notion of the "one best way". The forms of science and technology I am addressing in this book are predominantly those which have arisen within the context of those nations which had, or subsequently acquired a Christian, Jewish type of religion. Those are religions in which it is assumed that human beings have a right to dominate and exploit nature as they wish and that they are above nature since they are Godlike. Significantly, both of these regard themselves as being the one true religion and so we find the Catechism certainty for example of the assertion "The One True Catholic and Apostolic Church".

Our Science and Technology, which I suggest has arisen primarily within those cultures, also has as its central kernal the notion of the One Best Way. Many techniques in mathematics are based on processes of regression. That is to say, one arrives at a set of characteristics and by using the mathematics of regression these can be refined further and further, always reducing the range of possibilities and gradually converging and correcting to the "one best way". It is an interesting and powerful mathematical technique, useful in a number of specific applications but quite disastrous if one seeks to elevate this to a universal principle for the long term development of our society. Underlying it is the rather dangerous notion that diversity is a problem and that analysis will enable us to select from a range of alternatives that which is the optimum. Once optimised, by its own definition it should not be changed and thereby great rigidity and inflexibility is introduced.

I will seek to show that this philosophy is all pervasive in Western society and finds eloquent expressions in the factory model of organisation. That model is best expressed by Taylor, the founder of Scientific Management. It was his view that given any particular labour process, one could analyse it in such a fashion as to work out the best way of doing it. Once this started, those involved should blindly follow this One Best Way: "In my system, the workman is told precisely what he is to do and how he is to do it, and any improvements made on the instructions given to him is fatal to success". He also suggested that those most suitable to the acceptance of these ideas were those which "more closely resemble the ox, than any other kind".

I have demonstrated that these concepts have now spread to the areas of intellectual and creative work. I wish to suggest the blind unthinking application of these techniques will indeed reduce people to ox-like behaviour, and to passive, zombie-like behaviour as technologies and systems act upon them rather than the other way round. And so we find on all sides the standardisation of procedures, products and people. Let me emphasise that as an engineer, I am deeply aware of the use of standardisation.

The EEC's proposed integration from 1992 raises in a very overt way the issues of the "One Best Way". A basic issue is whether integration will in fact mean a simulation or whether integration will be more creatively interpreted as facilitating the interaction of different cultures and traditions. If we have a United States of Europe, in the cultural and social sense in which we think of the United States of America, then the danger is that Europe will become a sort of melting pot.

In the past, it could be argued that such a simulation did at least provide for greater productive cohesion at a time when mass production held sway worldwide and in consequence, US Corporations, and more recently Japanese ones, could dominate markets worldwide. However, given energy and material constraints, there are good grounds for believing that that form of industrial and cultural infrastructure may have run its course, and may now begin to be counterproductive.

The FAST Report: "European Competitiveness in the 21st Century: The Integration of Work, Culture and Technology" suggests that societies are going to have to move from economy of scale to economy of scope. If that is the case, diversity may well come into its own. The Report states: "However, the cultural richness and variety in Europe and a generally more creative spirit which has in the past made concerted focused approaches to industrial development rather difficult, have begun to appear more like strengths rather than weaknesses". It is, of course, extremely hard to assess the retrospective economic merits of different cultures in different situations in different times. It is clear however, that collaboration, cultural sophistication and creativity in the wider sense, are advantageous in post industrial society.

It is for this reason that Europe must not become a "melting pot", as the United States has become. Its regional and cultural variety will produce the basis for addressing diversified markets and responding to the demands of product variety. Given the environmental and energy constraints, different types of products meeting different needs will be essential. Diversified cultures should result in products which are specific to particular areas and the needs of those areas. Such products would also make better use of local materials. Each diversified culture gives a different background against which to view the design of new products and the use of different materials. This would mean in fact, not only diversified but distributed manufacturing and economic activities. This will run counter to the tendency of the 'one best way' to concentrate economic activities in particular regions. In consequence of this, the Report expresses concern that we may see polarisations of activity similar to those which we saw in each of the individual nation states previously. Thus, in the United Kingdom, one might say they were concentrated around London, Birmingham, Manchester and Newcastle in a sort of Y shape with Belfast and Glasgow as other centres and with the population being driven from Scotland, Ireland and Wales to seek employment in those areas of concentration.

There are now real fears that as a result of the inbuilt notion of the 'one best way', there will be concentrations of activity at the macro level in areas of Europe, and in consequence of this, there will begin to be defined a periphery which can be described geographically, culturally and economically. If we view it geographically (and cultural and economic peripheral effects tend in any case to follow) the new periphery in Europe could include all of Greece, all of Portugal, Southern Italy, Denmark, perhaps the Northern part of Germany as a result of the decline in shipbuilding and heavy industries, the North of England and all of Ireland. Yet it is precisely in these areas that some of the oldest and richest cultures in Europe exist – the Greek culture, the Scandinavian culture and the Celtic culture.

The Report therefore advocates that new technologies be used to diffuse economic and other activities outwards such that people in these regions will have an active economic basis around which their languages and cultures can continue to develop and can be truly living languages. The Report goes as far as to suggest that we shall have to facilitate the cultural and industrial renaissance right across Europe.

It would be particularly contradictory if, precisely at the historical stage when new technologies allow the distribution of activities, cultures should be seen to die because their people are required to gravitate to centres of economic concentration.

In the distributed systems proposed in the EEC Report, facilities exist for language exchanges, thus small co-operatives, or units working say in Greece, could work with their colleagues in Denmark, each of them using their own native local language. Machine translations would, in the first instance, give the gist of the matter under consideration, with a perhaps 90% accurate translation. If it then transpires that a more accurate one is required, the skilled human translators could fine-tune the rough work done with the machine. This in itself would provide a good human/machine symbiosis, but at the same time would also support the retention and development of the language and cultures in the individual regions.

CHAPTER 8

WAYS OF KNOWING

I have visited Japan on a number of occasions during recent years. I am associated with some universities there and have given a number of lecture series.

I usually try to start my lectures with a few remarks in Japanese which, although long rehearsed, are painfully stumbling and woefully inadequate. They are at least an attempt, however feeble, to show respect for a language and culture which I do not understand, before I embark upon my unintentional campaign of cultural imperialism by delivering my lectures in English. Since the substance of these talks is in the main, scientific and technical, they are usually well understood by those present.

I serve on the scientific board for a Japanese research project and am an adviser to a major Japanese corporation. In these activities too, the working medium is spoken and written English. My book *Architect or Bee?* has been translated into Japanese by Professor Fumihiko Satofuka and Hiroshima Sato. We discussed how best to convey the ethos of the book's central ideas into not only a different language but one located in a very different culture. Even the title of the book did not find easy expression in Japanese.

One was not just dealing with equivalent sets of words, but rather finding ways to encapsulate concepts and ideas in a culture, and a way of viewing and understanding the world which is very different from our own.

These interactions provide me with a miniscule keyhole view on those complex historical and cultural processes that have resulted in present day Japanese society. I cannot therefore profess any expertise in Japanese culture, indeed I must unfortunately admit to my lack of knowledge of it. However my interaction with Japanese culture, and my working with Japanese colleagues has allowed me to think anew about some of the issues facing us in Western industrial society. I have for example, been at quite high level meetings where discussions have proceeded in a convoluted and apparently leisurely fashion for a number of hours. Although this was being translated for me, I felt that I was clearly missing something, particularly when the meeting concluded and apparently no decisions had been made. Given my background in European industry I naturally took it that the interpreter had succeeded in missing some vital decisions since to me it seemed unthinkable that leading people should be brought together from several different parts of Japan and several different research projects and yet no decision should have been attempted, much less made. When I pursued this further it was explained to me "No there wasn't a decision. We do not celebrate decisions in the way you do in Europe. We are far more concerned at meetings of this kind with transmitting an ethos since ethos is not quantifiable" and its significance in a nation which is so technologically advanced did surprise me. I was beginning to encounter different ways of knowing or beginning to see 'the different faces' of understanding and meaning. On another occasion I was describing our work within the EEC FAST Programme to provide distributed systems to support variety in different parts of Europe. A profound discussion ensued as to the nature of diversity. In the course of this, an academic colleague, a Professor of the

History of Science and Technology, suggested gently and supportively that I appear to be talking about diversity on a horizontal axis where perhaps the more interesting approach might be to view diversity on a vertical axis.

In a few brief words he had revealed the latent shadow of my one dimensional man. In Osaka I was priveliged to be invited to the home of a Japanese colleague. It normally takes quite some time before this honour is bestowed. It was indeed an extraordinary experience. On all previous occasions I had met my colleague in the context of his international business environment. At my first meeting in the office block in Osaka, I had expected in a European sense that we would get down to it immediatley but there was firstly the tea drinking ceremony. In the course of this there was the convoluted and apparentley diversionary form of discussion. Apart from this, the discussion is as it may have been in Europe or in the United States. He was dressed in a well cut Western suit, was business-like, efficient, courteous and alarmingly well briefed about the project under consideration. My meeting with him at his home constituted a transformation. I took a taxi to his home in surburban Osaka and he met me in the garden in ceremonial robes. His family likewise were dressed in their robes so that I too might shed the outside world. I was given a traditional Japanese oath of welcome. There was traditional Japanese food prepared, served and eaten in a Japanese fashion.

The conversation was of other times, other values and other dimensions of human understanding. Following the meal we sat in the garden where we listened to the crickets and spoke about man in nature. I found it hard to equate the person before me with the high pressure executive I knew in downtown Osaka. It did however take one further event to bring home to me fully the point about diversity in a vertical axis. In the course of my visits and at international conferences, I have come to know a Japanese colleague who is an applied scientist of international reputation. Although the organisational aspects of his laboratory would differ from that of a similar institute in Germany or the United States. The equipment, methods of research and the findings are as they might be in a laboratory elsewhere. He is, to all intents and purposes, a Western scientist.

In the course of our discussions about Japanese culture, language and religious forms, he told me he was participating in a public religious festival which I might find interesting. I attended and was frankly amazed to see him participate, appropriately clad in ancient religious ritualistic costume. It seemed to me almost impossible to imagine a European scientist taking part in such rituals which would be seen as a form of superstition – as mystical, spiritual and subjective. I mentioned this to him and he explained quite simply: "I am able one day to function as a scientist and another day to be religious, or for that matter something else". It suddenly occurred to me that Western science and technology, which developed within our Western cultures, is understood and interpreted in such a way as to assume the capability of a complete description, a description of issues and materials and processes which, by virtue of being scientific and therefore 'fundamental', is so exact and so complete as to render irrelevant, or more particularly fallacious, any other form of explanation. Thus it would follow that to be a scientist, to have scientific rational explanations would of necessity mean that it would at the best be illogical to function at a level which involved belief, as distinct from proof. Subjective considerations as distinct from objective ones. This form of outlook now so pervasive in Western society is in fact a form of intellectual and cultural totalitarianism. It can accept only one level of description or knowing – the scientific definition and by virtue of its own inbuilt values it eliminates all others which do not accord with its own criteria.

So science and technology does not give us yet another way of knowing the world – it gives us the only way of knowing the world. Since a very early age at school, I have on a simple and subjective level found such a framework of totalitarian explanation unacceptable. What I am talking about is a sense in which the forms of scientific explanation and the ideological completeness which we believe surrounds it destroys that part of our humanity and of ourselves which allows us to understand matters at several different levels. What we are witnessing is the one best way on a massive and all pervasive scale. I am suggesting that a scientific explanation, unless it is seen as just one other and additional form of explanation and fits into a grander totality, will actually diminish rather than enhance our understanding of matters. I well recall the bitter disappointment I experienced by this form of unidimensional explanation when as a child of perhaps 11 or 12 I learned about the operation of the human eye. I had up till then thought of eyes as "Windows of the Soul". I had read stories of eyes burning with anger, of eyes melting into tears of sadness. I had read poems of eyes that appealed and eyes that longed and now I was told, the eye is simply an optical system. What I am attempting to describe is a way of knowing which subordinates, subverts, destroys and eliminates other ways of knowing when it should simply be another frequency of our understanding. I am not for one moment suggesting that the description of the eye as an optical system is not important. The knowledge we now have of the eyes optical system is of vital importance to opticians and surgeons. Miracles of modern science which allow the blind to see, would not be possible without laser surgical techniques which require a deep understanding of the eye's functioning at a scientific level. But in our humanity, we are more than opticians, we are colleagues, friends, husbands, wives, sons, daughters, negotiators, bluffers, dramatists who in our day-to-day exchanges with fellow human beings, need to be able to read their expressions to see if what we are doing is angering them, reducing them to tears, stimulating their interest. As theatre-goers or as cinema audiences, we need to be chilled by the eye's expression in an Eisenstein film or touched by the loving affection between Romeo and Juliet. The same may be said of clouds. There is the scientific or meterological description of them. In this case a cloud is simply a large collection of tiny H_2O droplets suspended in air in a form which is too light to fall to earth as rain. Clouds whose bases are below 200 metres are low clouds, those between 200 and 600 are medium clouds and those whose bases are over 600 metres are high clouds. There are amalgamations of these, and thus clouds with bases of perhaps about 500 metres but whose tops extend to the high cloud brackets, are known as cumulus or cumulonimbus. In lower clouds there are strato cumulus, stratus and nimbo stratus. If the under part of the layer is broken up, these parts may be called fractostratus. The medium clouds altocumulus and altostratus. Altocumulus is similar to stratocumulus.

There are three types of high clouds – Cirrus, Cirrocumulus and Cirrostratus. And so one could go on taking such descriptions from any simple book on weather or meteorology. But this understanding of clouds is different from that of artists who have perhaps been intrigued by the towering shapes so beautifully painted by Paul Henry and others, as merely another cumulonimbus. I still recall lying in meadows for hours on end during seemingly infinitely long summer days, vying with playmates to see who could identify and describe the most interesting shapes in the clouds. Malachy O'Keefe's grey mare with floating mane made frequent appearances. Arms with bursting muscles would float by and as the great panorama swept in over the West coast, this marvellous theatre of the sky produced for us giants, skeletons, bulging faces and the more observant amongst us, such as Tom Murphy, could identify John Connolly's anvil.

The farmers could read from the shape and direction of the clouds, if and when rain would come and Cirrocumulus or Altocumulus were not those strange names at all but the mackerel sky and generations of observers of such a sky confirmed without great statistical analysis that our little chant was usually correct: "Mackerel sky, mackerel sky, not long wet, not long dry".

And then there were the theatrical lighting effects. Most spectacular of all, the underlighting of the clouds from the reflection of the atlantic. Science should enhance rather than eliminate such imagery and understanding.

Consider a scientific description of a hazlenut. In a scientific sense it is complete in itself. The material scientist in some remote area of the world where hazlenuts do not grow and who has never seen one, will nonetheless have the same and complete scientific understanding as a scientist in Europe. But another way of knowing the hazlenut will be, as Polanyi put it, an operating entity. It may connotate for us images of childhood when there were seemingly inpenetrable hazel bushes with their well known characteristic shape and form where a small green object was gradually transformed in the energy absorbing warmth, firstly into its familiar shape and then gradually assuming its brown outer colour. This marked for us the change of the seasons and also the time at which one set forth in gangs to collect them.

Hazlenuts could also help to tell fortunes. One would place the hazlenuts on the edge of the stove and whoever's nut exploded first would be the first to leave home. They could connotate images of rocks emerging in a sea of chocolate in those delightfully fattening milk chocolate hazlenut bars, be transformed and restructured into the filling of a chocolate nut that even had a shape like the original.

More and more members of our industrial society will come to know materials at the level of their material science description. It clearly will be of scientific advantage as we develop new materials and new surface finishes, new composites, semiconducting polymers, but it should only complement our other understanding of materials. At the particle level a piece of oak in its abstract description is very much like a piece of beech and we already have those who cannot see the wood for the molecules. Indeed, at the particle level, all materials are very much the same, they just have slightly different configurations. We fail to see a piece of wood as part of an operating entity.

The tree which grew from an acorn, struggled with other plants to survive, extended roots to draw in water, extended branches to reach toward the light and, in the process, formed that beautiful wood which is a delight to see when fashioned by a craftsman.

All materials begin to be the same except for different particle configurations if we know them only at the scientific level. Particles which constitute one human being are the same as the particles of another. They are slightly differently configured and more or less of them are embodied to make us large, small, black, white, blonde or whatever. The brain too viewed thus is simply a highly interesting configuration of such particles. One brain as much as the other, variously programmed. And so even the characteristics which can make us attractive personalities, vicious personalities, composers, writers, craftsmen, all can be seen as nothing more than a simple configuration of particles. In such descriptions we know more about materials and people at one level and we know precious little about them at another.

In a society increasingly organised on such scientific principles, the ecological processes by which materials develop will be less understood. So too will the significance of individual character commitment and intentionality. All will be a grey mass of interacting particles. Exact technical and scientific decriptions now begin to be the order of the day. In computer based motorway layout for example, cartographic and other descriptions can be input by a three dimensional co-ordinate which define contours and shapes. Those in remote city offices, armed with such exact knowledge and scientific descriptions presume to know that terrain. I cannot however accept that their knowledge of it is more profound and more important than a farmer who paints its fields brown with a plough, with the artist who immortalises it in a painting, or the hunter or fisherman who gently teases trout from its streams.

Do not argue the dominance of one knowledge over the other. I simply suggest that we need both and many more. It is precisely this arid description of terrain which I would suggest with its computer aided planning and modelling has done so much damage in urban planning and city development. The idea of human scale, harmony of building, the very atmosphere and life of a city required that those planning these things are intimately in contact with the terrain and the people who will reside upon it, that they understand the significance of squares and meeting points to create a community atmosphere and that they have seen the shadow of the building as sun sets. The realism and exactness of computer aided design systems could, if properly used, actually enhance our capacity to know, understand and hence improve our enviroment but the values embodied within them are that of the rationalist, productionist model.

Can any of us, even in our wildest dreams, really think of a computer aided design system which would result in a city devoid of roads or traffic built on water and called Venice. Even the cities that we know, we know not just in terms of the number of buildings, their height and the metric arrangements – we know them also in the sense of their history and the events that have taken place there, the sieges of the cities, the triumphant entry of conquerors. The image those conquerors have imposed upon the city and its dwellings, the purpose of its fortifications, the significance of its rivers and location, the people who live there as if the cities say to us: "I am a part of all that I have known". A city being physical and being constructed of given materials could be seen to fit into a scientific and technical description. At one level, indeed, such a description can be provided, but a city means more than that. The voices of its past speak out to us, certain buildings and locations have particular significances for us, others fade into a hazy background. Routes we walk bring back memories of earlier events and colleagues and companions at that time. To the historian of national liberation movements, Dublin might be seen as the city of 1916, the focal point upon the GPO and the proclamation there of the Provisional Government of the Irish Republic declaring that it will cherish "all the children of the nation equally". For the lover of James Joyce, there is a different way of knowing the city

> "Joyce was alive and this was his river. The whispering city repeated over and over the words and phrases he took from it once. Wherever we went in Dublin, he had been there before us. Odd how the years long rain pounds on the streets, but never clears his shabby bootprints from the stone."
>
> *Poems for James Joyce* p.44

We, all of us as individuals, have a unique and different view. The richness of our humanity has been enhanced by science and technology, which is but one product of the delinquent genius. In the last three or four hundred years it has come to dominate our thinking, our outlook, our relationships and the product of our own genius is assuming such awesome proportions that it is now disabling us mentally, culturally and socially.

CHAPTER 9

THE SHOUT OF JOY

In the narrow, rationalistic, technological, programmable world I have been talking about, we are continually required to deny the reality of our own experiences. This takes the form of a post hoc rationalisation of what we have experienced. In order for it to be significant, we are required to show that it is the outcome of a series of logical sequential steps which led to an end result. I am not here suggesting that such logical sequential steps do not have their part to play nor am I suggesting they are insignificant. I am however suggesting that they are but a tiny part of the totality of human experience. However even in research and development laboratories where large groups of teams are working together innovations, concepts for new ideas are still based on the insights of individuals and that those insights and ideas are the stimulus for a research and development activity or for the identification of a product which may ultimately result.

Since, however, insight like imagination and intuition is not quantifiable, is not predictable, and is not repeatable, its significance is always underplayed if not totally denied. This denial is built in at the very root of our scientific methodology, a methodology which is dominating our thinking in all fields of human endeavour. We all of us tend to construct an edifice of post hoc scientific explanation since deep down we have a fear of that uncertainty and that unpredictability which is at the root of intuition, imagination and creativity. Let us suppose for a moment that we encounter a great and acclaimed scientific thinker who has codified the laws of thought and in doing so has laid the basis for the use of mathematics as a model of thinking. Let us suppose that this great scientific thinker has produced a philosophical and scientific framework for rationality. Let us suppose that following profound scientific and philosophical discussion, these ideas were found to be internally consistent within a logical framework. Let us further suppose that this framework was the basis for mathematical modelling of thought processes which showed that thinking could be modelled and these models could be based on mathematics. Let us then suppose that this work had been massively funded worldwide to the level of billions of dollars annually and all of this work demonstrated in its own self consistent terms that there were logical, scientific and mathematical ways of modelling thought processes. Suppose then we were to meet the originator of this huge and mathematical scientifical edifice of analysis and we asked them how they arrived at their concept of this scientific construct. We would be alarmed if they told us " I was told by an angel". Our alarm would not be lessened if they added that they were told by an angel in a dream, yet it would seem that that was exactly what did happen. On the night of November 10th 1619 Daca had a series of three dreams in which the angel of truth revealed to him a secret which "would lay the basis of a new method of understanding and a new science".

The significance of such dreams, revelations, brainwaves, insights, sparks of imagination are usually carefully omitted from post hoc analysis. It seems to be slightly more acceptable to refer to them in the context of the arts. To do so is indeed of longstanding. Socretes pointed out: "The authors of these great poems which we admire do not attain to excellence, to the rules of any art. They utter their beautiful melodies of verse in a state of inspiration as it were possessed by a spirit of their own". (*The unknown guest* p. 7)

Stephen Spender, whilst emphasising the importance of "Work" on a poem, states: "Inspiration is the beginning of a poem and it is also its final goal ... My own experience is certainly that of a line or a phase or a word or something still vague, a dim cloud of an idea which I feel must be condensed into a shower of words".

He points out that Paul Valéry speaks of the "una ligna donne/e" of a poem. One line is given to the poet by God or by nature. The rest he has to discover for himself. The significance of childhood and early images is emphasised when Spender says: "All poets have this highly developed apparatus of memory and they are usually aware of experiences which happened to them at the earliest ages and which retain their pristine significance throughout their lives" One might refer to Dante's meeting with Beatrice which became the symbol around which the devine comedy crystallised. The experiences of nature which form the subjects of Wordsworth's poetry were an extension of a childhood vision of natural presences which surrounded the boy Wordsworth. The decision in his later life to live in the Lake District was one based on the desire to live on those childhood memories which were the most important experiences in his poetry. One might cite Rilke's notion of words rising up and imposing themselves upon him and they being "the most mysterious". One might cite Mozart's famous letter, although some tend to discount it or Tchaikovsky for whom music is "a more subtle medium in which to translate the 1000 shifting moments in the mood of a soul". One might fill many moments with examples of the importance of inspiration, mood, insight, imagination and that inner creative voice which so often sparks our imagination in the most unlikely places and at the most extraordinary times. A professor of anatomy at Harvard summed it up succinctly over 100 years ago when he said: "We all of us have a double who is wiser and better than we are and who puts thoughts into our heads and words into our mouth". This double he describes as:

> "A creating and informing spirit which is with us and not of us, is recognised everywhere here and in story life. It is the Zeus that kindled the rage of Achilles; it is the muse of Homer – it is the demon of Socrates, it is the inspiration of the see-er – it is the smoking devil that whispers to Margaret as she kneels at the altar – it is the hobgoblin who cries "Sell him, Sell him" in the ear of John Bunyan; it shaped the forms that formed the soul of Michelangelo when he saw the figure of the great law giver in the yet unhewn marble in the dome of the world's yet unbuilt Basilika against the black horizon. It comes to the least of us as a voice that will be heard; it tells us that we must believe; it frames our sentences; it lends a sudden gleam of elegance to the dummest of us all."[4]

It may be accepted that this inspiration and intuition is significant in the arts but has no place within the sciences, indeed with the technocratic reductionist thinking which now dominates western society. Little is done to provide an enviroment which stimulates the imagination and leads to creativity in its multivarious forms. Given the austere, logical, sequential, mathematical image of science, it is worth emphasising that creative scientists, with few exceptions, freely admit to the significance of intuition, insight, and imagination.

In the world of the reductionist, everything has to be made clear, specific and precise. There is no space for ambiguity, uncertainty or lack of clarity. The history of ideas suggests it is not as straightforward as that. Frequently it is some half-baked idea, some fuzzy correlation, a smell, a sound, that triggers the imagination and produces something of significance.

In the reductionist view, everything can be explained by scientific means. This means that every aspect of human behaviour must be explored and expressed scientifically. Our innermost thoughts, our likes, our dislikes, should all be made visible and explained.

Even our dreams will now be subjected to such scrutiny. Research is now taking place into what is known as 'lucid dreaming'. The object, as with most science and technology, is to achieve control. In a lucid dream you become conscious that you are dreaming and you take control. There has been developed the dreamlight, which it is held, will help people to have lucid dreams. In the 50's, psychologists rejected that notion, when electroencephalogram revealed the faces of sleep, especially REM (rapid eye movement) sleep, during which, if you wake somebody they are likely to report that they have been dreaming. The muscles are relaxed to the point of paralysis, the brain is active but the sleeper is difficult to wake.

It was held that it would be impossible to be conscious during such a dreaming state. Development suggests that by using REM techniques, it is possible to know when one is dreaming and hence make estimates of the time of the dream.

It is said that this research will give insight into the ultimate human mystery, the brain, by identifying the range and location of its activities. It is believed that lucid dreaming will act as a bridge between the conscious and the sub-conscious, and that the work could have surgical as well as psychological benefits. It is suggested that the same parts of the brain are active in waking and sleeping. Tasks such as singing use the opposite half of the brain. Researchers have found that subjects signal from a dream that they are singing when in fact they are adding up. The same areas are active.

With the dreamlight, the eye movements are detected using personal computers which switch on flashing lights when the eye movements rapidly reach a certain point. It is hoped that eventually all the necessary circuitry will be incorporated in a pair of goggles. These are put on at bedtime and flash only when the subject is asleep and dreaming. The person can control the level of eye movements at which the light begins to flash.

Francis Crick, who won the Nobel Prize for his shared discovery of DNA, suggests there is a danger in this interfering with dreams. He believes that the function of dreams is forgetting, in which case it might be best that they are left alone. However, researchers working on the dreamlight are adamant that "its going to help people have lucid dreams and lucid dreams are good" (*Sunday Times*, June 6th, 1990).

In considering the work of scientists, engineers and mathematicians, it may seem sacrilegious to talk about something as introverted and personal as their "spirit", yet scientists them selves would go even further. Poincaré suggests it is necessary to "see what goes on in the very soul of the mathematician". To illustrate the point, he described how he discovered a number of mathematical theorems:

> "For 15 days I strove to prove that there could not be any functions like those I have since called Fuchsian functions. I

was then very ignorant. Every day I seated myself at my worktable, stayed an hour or two, tried a great number of combinations and reached no result. One evening, contrary to custom, I drank black coffee and could not sleep. Ideas rose in crowds. I felt them collide until pairs interlocked so to speak, making a stable combination. The next morning I had established the existence of a class of Fuchsian functions – those which come from the hypergeometric series. I had only to write out the results which took me but a few hours."

In extending this area of work, he likewise had further 'insights':

"The changes of travel made me forget my mathematical work. Having reached Coutances, we entered an omnibus to go to some place or another. At the moment I put my foot on the step the idea came to me without anything in my former thoughts seeming to have paved the way for it, that the transformations I had used to define the Fuchsian functions were identical with those of non-Euclidian geometry."

And without any notion that they may be connected to his preceding researches, he states:

"Disgusted with my failure. I spent a few days at the seaside and thought of something else. One morning walking on the bluff, the idea came to me with just the same idea of brevity, suddeness and immediate certainty, that the arithmetic transformations of intermediate, ternary quadratic forms were identical to those of non-Euclidian geometry."

I am not suggesting here that such sudden insights will come to just anybody. Clearly a deep knowledge of mathematics and the study of those subjects is a precondition for the ability to recognise such an insight when it occurs. The point I am making here, however, is that the mere possession of mathematical knowledge acquired in a systematic rule based way, is not the whole story.

Furthermore, such rule based systems do not take into account that which goes on in the subconscious. Poincaré points out: "Most striking at first is this appearance of sudden illumination, a manifestation of long unconscious prior work. The role of this unconscious work in mathematical invention appears to me incontestable, and traces of it can be found in other cases where it is less evident".

The point I wish to emphasise here is that he repeatedly points out the importance of the emotional and the feeling in the context of mathematical creativity, and that which he called privileged unconscious phenomena:

> "Those susceptible to becoming conscious are those which directly or indirectly, affect most profoundly our emotional sensibility ... It may be surprising to see emotional sensibility evoked appros of mathematical demonstrations which it would seem can interest only the intellect. This would be to forget the feeling of mathematical beauty, of the harmony of numbers and forms, of geometric elegance. This is a true aesthetic feeling that all real mathematicians know and surely it belongs to emotional sensibility."

Computerised systems, and those which are rule-based by definition, lack this true "aesthetic feeling" and "emotional sensibility". Thus in spite of the speed, consistency and repeatability, we should not think of them in the sense of human progress and creativity, as superior to human beings but rather they should be treated as support systems and tools which support the creative emotions of human beings. Sadly, most scientists seem unwilling to admit to the significance of this emotional and subjective dimension of their work. It is perhaps a measure of the extent to which they are themselves victims of the dominant technocratic ideology. It is also surprising that a profession which prides itself on its rationality and objectivity so often seeks to deny the truth of the creative process.

They do seem to be victims of their own propoganda and determined to imply that scientific advance, the emergence of mathematical theorems and the invention of new products are based on a scientific method which involves inductive reasoning, logical sequential steps, in a word something which is rigidly codified and leaves little space for our humanity. This in turn gives rise to the notion that scientific "training" at school and university should be based on hard facts, methods, procedures and that excitement and motivation have little place in the preparation of scientists. It means that that part of us which is the essence of our humanity has little space within the sciences and that creative people should find vent for their capabilities elsewhere.

In reality, science should be an exciting as well as a demanding area of study which has space for both the subjective and the objective, the inductive and the deductive. Scientists actually succeed in alienating potential students of their courses with the image they create of their profession. Medua points out that if one really presses a scientist, they would "Probably mumble something about induction" and "establishing the laws of nature"; but if anyone working in a laboratory professed to be trying to establish the laws of nature by induction we should begin to think that he was overdue for leave. It is most unlikely that anything more than a tiny minority of theorems were ever arrived at, "discovered" merely by the existence of deductive reasoning. Most of them entered the mind by processes of the kind vaguely called intuition. Deduction or logical derivation came later, to justify or falsify what was in the first place an inspiration or an intuitive belief. This is seldom apparent from mathematical writings because mathematicians take pains to ensure that it should not be.

I would go so far as to say there is an intellectual dishonesty amongst such professions. If they wish to be dishonest with each other, that is up to them. What is unacceptable is that their dishonesty is used as part of a wider process which is increasingly imposing on society this narrow mechanistic view of the world. Much more needs to be done by scientists themselves to have the courage to allow their inner voices to speak. On the occasions when they do, we get some of that human freshness which is almost poetic. The discoverer of insulin, Sir Frederick Banting, says that ideas come "when the imagination is allowed to run riot on the problems that block the progress of research, when the huge stones of scientific fact are turned over and fitted in so that the mosaic figure of truth, designed by mother nature long ago, may be formed from the chaos".[7]

It is important that we freely admit to Ampere's "shout of joy" when he finally found the solution to a problem he had firstly formulated some seven years earlier. Our science and technology would be the richer, and our courses in those subjects would attract the more creative, sensitive members of society, if they included accounts of Faraday having a vision of tubes which "rose up before him like things" or admit with Carl Gauss:

" ... come to me when my mind was fatigued or when I was at

my working table. They came particularly readily during the slow ascent of wooded hills on a sunny day."[9]

In all of these cases, it was attributes other than just technical and scientific competence that appeared to have facilitated the 'Eureka' step. Certainly, there was a sensitivity to a problem or an issue. There is usually much fringe consiousness of the subject area but above all there is imagination and it is this which in many ways defines our humanity. Gaining the power to accumulate experience and to reason was not enough to make him man. Another quality was necessary – the grcat gift of imagination. "This is perhaps mans most distinctive trait for it makes possible his creativity."[10] The dominant tendancy in our society is to deny the significance of the subjective, the imaginative and seek to replace that by the scientific and the quantifiable rather than to complemenmt it by this rational dimension.

I do believe the long term implications for our species are serious indeed. We have associated the ascent of man with imagination and creativity. It seems not unreasonable to assume that we can associate the decline of man with the lack of these attributes.

CHAPTER 10

TIME OUT OF MIND

As a species, we suffer from many forms of illness, both physical and mental. Many of these we categorise, analyse and devise methods of treatment. It is usually easier to recognise the manifestation of physical illnesses. The mental ones are often elusive to the point of slipping through the crude net of recognition. Alternatively, they insinuate themselves into our consciousness in such a gradual and covert way, that like perfect camouflage they merge into the background of our consciousness, so completely that we are oblivious to their existence.

Such an elusive malady is one I call Acute Narcissus Technology Syndrome (ANTS). Although it exists on an epidemic scale in Western society, it is unrecognised and therefore not surprisingly untreated. Fragmented manifestations of it are treated in conjunction with other illnesses. Half those in hospital in the United States are there for non-physical illnesses. The borderline between coping and non-coping is modulated with a sort of Valium feedback. Psychiatrists' couches groan under the production-line stream of patients. There are stress relieving holidays, therapeutic sports, biofeedback mechanisms and mindbending devices are distributed like confetti. Yet one of the contributory factors, Acute Narcissus Technology Syndrome (ANTS), continues to inflict its damage on industrial society unabated.

ANTS compels us to think of ourselves as machines, to act as machines, to assess ourselves as machines and to communicate as machines. Since we are not machines, this grotesque masquerade is deeply debilitating. Many and varied are the influences which inflict this malady upon us.

My colleague, Professor Rosenbrock, has brilliantly described those present modes of scientific thought which impose a belief that man is a machine, and therefore as humans, we can contribute nothing which cannot be contributed just as well by machines. The devastation this causes our self-image should not be underestimated. As Rosenbrock shows, this belief arises from four centuries of a science based on strictly causal explanations. He shows how our world might equally be interpreted in terms of purpose, and how this would profoundly change our attitude to ourselves and to nature. To take that step, it will be necessary to courageously break the mirror of our technological narcissism. I hold that we create technologies as distorted mirror images of ourselves. We then gaze mesmerized, dazzled at those technological images and within them, see ourselves reflected as machines. Our consciousness is numbed by what we see. This is narcissism in both the classical and modern sense.

The young Narcissus you will recall, mistook his own image in the water for another person. He was so captivated by the image that he was oblivious to other influences. He was separated even from his own speech. Thus when the nymph Echo tried to win his love with the resonance of his own speech, this too was in vain.

I have frequently suggested that our technologies reduce us to a mere machine appendage, act upon us, and lock us into a form of closed system. McLuhan, in his *Understanding Media*, describes the predicament of

Narcissus in similar terms: "This extension of himself by mirror, numbed his perceptions until he became the servo-mechanism of his own extended, or repeated image ... He was numb. He had adapted to the extension of himself and had become a closed system".

I have often referred to our technologies as bludgeoning our common sense into silence and numbing our senses. Indeed, to the alarm of some of my engineering colleagues I have referred to technology in its present form as a drug. Narcotic does mean 'numbness' and narcotic comes from the Greek 'narcosis'. However, it was from Narcissus that we get the word narcosis.

Technologies do reflect the human being or some aspect of his or her capacities directly, and in an external form. That is to say that we confer life on a machine. We try to do this in our own image and then we look at the machine and think of ourselves in terms of the capacities and attributes of that machine. This may all seem a bit elusive and difficult to grasp, so let me therefore give an example of what I mean. I suggested at the beginning of this book that we have tried to mirror in machines, some of the capabilities of ourselves.

I suggested that we designed machines that "walk", machines that "feed" and now, machines that "think". Let us consider the first of these machines that "walk". A good example of these are the clockwork mechanisms which have been developed in Europe for hundreds of years. They range from large mechanisms such as the great clock in Prague where figures emerge from the belfry and move around striking the bells, to the modern glockenspiel mechanisms, where again figures emerge and play a variety of tunes on a range of suspended bells.

At the other end of the scale, there are the delicate and ornate miniature mechanisms with figures of ballerinas, no higher than a matchbox, who not only "walk" but "dance", including complicated ballet routines on a small stage which has a built-in "music box" providing accompaniment. Other mechanisms provide for Mozart-like figures sitting at tiny pianos and playing a range of quite complicated tunes. The human ingenuity and craft skills which were lavished on these magnificent mechanisms are an elegant tribute to man's creativity and artistry.

The creation of movement – breathing life into objects – is a dream as old as man himself. Automats have existed for thousands of years, but the development of mechanical timekeeping in the 13th Century, bestowed upon them the gift of life. The old watchmakers' tools may have been rudimentary but with great patience, divine skill and loving care, they succeeded in creating spring driven mechanisms whose movement gave an appearance of life itself.

Snuggling in the mountains in the middle of the Swiss watchmaking area is the Museum at Chateau des Monts du Locle. It is a mecca of clockwork mechanisms. There is some piece there to amaze and delight the most naive child and the most sophisticated adult. A clock whose face encompasses a tiny forge in which the rhythm of the blacksmith's hammer strikes out the seconds on his anvil. There is a village scene with a young peasant woman pumping water while her dog energetically laps it up from a bucket. Not to be outdone, another master clockmaker has a bridge with figures walking over it whilst below there flows water out of which fish appear to entice the fisherman on the bank who vigourously casts his line in vain. In a remarkable display of locomotion, there are caterpillars of actual size that creep along the surface. There are reptiles and animals with skins of gold, veins of pearls and rubies for their eyes, but all with mechanical hearts.

Then there are the singing birds. Henri-Louis Jaquet-Droz was the first creator of such birds, inscribing on their mechanical memories, the birdsongs typical of the Jura forest. The bird flutters its wings so realistically that one is surprised it doesn't take to the air whilst it sings a song created by a minute pair of bellows and a slide whistle completely concealed in the tree trunk on which the bird has alighted. Then there are the creations of Carl Fabergé, that extraordinary jeweller to the Russian Imperial Court. One of his masterpieces is a mauve enamelled egg with diamond ribbons. It is but the size of an ordinary egg yet when opened there emerges a swan a mere inch high which is capable of 'swimming' across a glass surface whilst its tiny neck rotates to quizzically inspect its surroundings and its wings move majestically in Swan Lake-like fashion. This egg, with its active embryo, was a gift to empress Alexandra to mark the old Easter tradition in spectacular fashion. There is too the minute peacock which fans its feathers in arrogant strutting fashion and then gently folds them so that it can be returned to the crystal egg, which was a present from Nicholas II to Empress Maria.

But pride of place for me goes to the minute figure in gold of an old woman by a Bavarian artist craftsman. Her aged figure bowed over with the ravages of time, moves with the aid of her two walking sticks. She does really walk in the sense that her tiny feet take actual steps, whilst her hands move the walking sticks forward in a manner that is bewilderingly realistic. This priceless collection invites us to marvel at one of the pinnacles of the craft tradition.

But these artefacts are not just wonders of precision engineering, craft skill and design, they are also works of art. Future generations will measure the level of our civilisation and sophistication as they read from the delicate movements of their mechanisms and the artistry of their decoration the cultural nuances of the societies which gave rise to them. This was the genius of our species being expressed in but one of our species' marvellous creations. But the delinquent aspect of our species was also at work. As we gazed in wonder at these mechanisms, we saw Narcissus-like, a reflection of ourselves but like Narcissus, we did not recognise it for what it was and we began to think of ourselves as machines. Drawings began to depict human limbs as operating mechanisms. Muscles and sinews were seen as the levers and pushrods of the automata. In discourse, and in philosophical reasoning, the human being is thought of more and more as a form of machine, and these thought processes, these inner reflections, found expression in 1637, when in his *Discourse on Method, Optics, Geometry, and Meteorology*, Descartes refers to the human body as a machine. This would appear to be the first time in history that such a clear comparison is made. Descartes said:

> "and this will not seem strange to those who, knowing how many different automata or moving machines can be made by the industry of man without employing in so doing, more than a very few parts in comparison to the great multitude of bones, muscles, nerves, arteries, veins or other parts which are to be found in the body of each animal. From this aspect, the body is regarded as a machine which, having been made by the hands of God, is incomparably better arranged, and possesses in itself movements which are much more admirable than any of those which can be invented by man".

Since that time, the notion of the human being as a machine has developed in parallel with forms of technology which perceive the human being as a machine and seek to create in machines 'human attributes'. As it is not possible to reproduce in a machine, those particularly human attributes of imagination, intentionality, humour or the subjective aspects, all those things which cannot be reduced to rules and therefore amenable to machine-like behaviour are increasingly portrayed in Western Industrial Society as being at the best irrelevant, or at the worst dangerous human illusions.

But clocks and timing mechanisms brought in their wake even more significant psychological changes than those of thinking of ourselves as machines. It produced a different concept of time. For me, the clock has always been a more significant agent of change than the printing press or even the steam engine. Only the computer, I believe, will surpass it in its significance.

Most of the technologies we develop are an attempt to extend our human capability. As a species we are relatively puny and slow. We can't fly and we don't swim all that well, but we are very ingenious. Early on when we couldn't lift heavy weights, we found that by using a lever we could broadly increase our lifting capability in proportion to the location of the fulcrum on the lever arm. Even when we could lift up weights using levers, our puny structure was not very good for bearing them along even if we gathered in large numbers, so we probably rolled weights along on logs and gradually evolved the wheel. We wished to expand into and stay in climates which up to then evolution had not suited us to cope with, so we extended our skin firstly by wearing the skins of other species and then gradually increasing the scope of our 'skin' by the production and use of clothes.

We were unwilling to accept our ability to view things

only within our own viewing distance so we developed telescopes to extend our eyes. When we found that our teeth and nails did not allow us to pierce, tear, cut and penetrate an extended range of materials, we used hand held stones with sharp edges and extended these with different forms of flint, and eventually we evolved a miriad of tools, knives of astonishing variety, spears, swords, axes of some 40 or 50 kinds, needles, saws, shears, scissors – the list seems endless. Likewise, our hands were not particularly good at scratching or removing materials so we developed pickaxes, files, carbonstones, spokeshaves, planes.

Complete books could be written on the development of any one of those lines of tools. They differ in shape, size, form, material, method of application and holding position. Complete crafts grew up through the use of special tools: we have stonecutters, stonemasons, carpenters, seamstresses. But however varied and diverse these tools and devices, all of them have one thing in common: they are essentially extensions of the human body and as such they can be classified as prosthetic – artificial limbs and organs. The clock, however, was a very different order of things.

The clock is an autonomous machine. It is true that it still embodied part of us in its early form in the sense that part of our energy was built into it. We wound up a spring or we pulled up a weight but once we released the mechanism, it displayed an independence of us as human beings. Beyond that, the clock does not represent man physically at all. Nor does it measure, move or form a physical entity, it measures time. But what is time? It is immaterial. It is a reflection of man's ideas, a mirror of a rational idea. That is the idea of an independent world of mathematically precise and measurable sequences.

Its introduction transformed society dramatically by instilling an awareness of a linear, progressive, sequential notion of time. It replaced the previous notion of time, which was an organic and cyclic perception. In consequence, rhythms of work and activity, independent of nature and of the weather, were gradually established. Surprisingly, some of these were in the monastery which became a sort of regularised praying machine. Bells rang to call the worshippers to Matins and Vespers irrespective of sunset or sunrise. 8 o'clock was 8 o'clock. Insofar as it was possible to be independent of nature, agricultural work within hearing distance of the bells began to be synchronised with 'time'. Up to then, and for some time after, activities may be said to have been based on task-related time. There was a time to harvest, a time to protect sheep (when they were lambing), a time to collect wool during the warm summer weather. The tasks were greatly influenced by nature. If it rained on a particular day, the task was postponed until another more appropriate day. All the older languages embodied sayings which told us that we had to rotate tasks to appropriate weather and conditions rather than to a fixed time.

There are parts of the world where those different perceptions of time still exist. Even in isolated communities in Europe, there are still enclaves that have not been entirely subordinated to the 'new time'. When Synge visited the Arran islands, he was surprised by the differing notions of time, its relation to the natural rhythms of work. In such natural rhythms, fishing boats are launched to attend the tides, furthermore one fishes when the shoals are in. Crops must be sown in spring and harvested in autumn. Cows have to be milked when their udders are full and sheep guarded when they are lambing. Synge pointed out:

"Few people however, are sufficiently used to modern time to understand in more than a vague way the convention of the hours, and when I tell them what o'clock it is by my watch, they are not satisfied and ask how long is left them before the twilight."

The changed notion of time transformed every aspect of our lives; not least within work itself. Previously, a worker might sell the product of his or her labour – a statue, a painting, a piece of cloth or a pair of shoes. Gradually, that method of exchange was transformed from selling the product of one's labour to selling one's labour time. So people were paid by the hour. That meant obsessional scrutiny on how the hour was spent. If people didn't work vigorously during the 'hour' they were sacked. Methods of assessing their activity during the hour developed. Organisational forms included supervisors, foremen and then the synchronisation of the production line itself. Unions went on strike to try and establish the 80 hour week, and recently, massive strikes took place in West Germany to reduce the week from 40 hour to 37.5 hours.

Within the work process itself, the German unions fought for work cycles no less than 90 seconds. In *Architect or Bee?* I have described agreements in the automotive industry in which the worker is subjected to the following time elements: Trips to the lavatory 1.62 minutes. It's computer precise. Not 1.6 or 1.7 but 1.62. For fatigue 1.3 minutes. Sitting down after standing too long 65 seconds. For monotony 35 seconds and so the grotesque litany goes on.

When we buy a record or a tape, apart from a statement of which piece of music is on it, we are given the time. We buy video tapes for 60 or 180 minutes, audio tapes for 60, 90 or 120 minutes. The times of individual pieces of music on a tape are given. Solicitors charge us by the hour. People synchronise their lives to accord with particular television programme times. Video recording is one attempt to escape the tyrany of time, but it is at the best, only a 'time shifter'. Theoretically at least, irrespective of the weather or the seasons of the year, work starts at a set time and finishes at a set time. Where minor concessions to this are made, it is called 'flexible time'. Those travelling to and from work each day work to a highly sunchronised time sequence. They leave home at a definite time, drive to the local station in (say) eight minutes, leave three minues to board the train (assuming it is on time!) travel into Paddington, know that they would get the Bakerloo line to connect them to Trafalgar Square and then there is six minutes walking time to the office. All of which will get them in at five minutes before nine assuming everything 'works normally'.

When we use the telephone we are charged by time on a sliding scale that also reflects distance. When we put on the light we are charged per kilowatt hour. When we go on a taxi journey the meter ticks away. Modern science, with its instruments which measure frequency, absorption times, decay times, would be quite impossible in its present form without time. Aircraft flight times are related to fuel consumption so that flying time over that planned can lead to a disaster. House alarm systems provide for 30 seconds in which to key in the code before the alarm is off.

We have not yet entirely succeeded in escaping from natural rhythms of time and task related ones. There are gestation times, female cycle times, and our circadian cycle times. Although different professions, crafts and occupations can exchange time for fixed amounts of money and although it is possible to exchange one currency for another, it is not possible to exchange one segment of time for another. To work on a nightshift is different from working during the day as our own circadian cycle will quickly make plain to us. If we fly to Tokyo we cannot simply exchange Tokyo time for London time. Our bodies will tell us that our sleeping time has been shifted.

It would not have been possible for those introducing the early clock mechanisms to have anticipated the dramatic and all pervasive consequences of their invention. As Shakespeare put it in *Macbeth*: "If you can look into the seeds of time and say which grain will grow and which will not". Nor am I suggesting that before the introduction of modern time, the quality of life was better. Only future generations can properly assess whether the material advantages afforded by high levels of synchronisation and the related co-ordination of events compensate for that which was replaced. Some already feel that it did not. Thus Weizenbaum says:

> "The clock created a new reality. This was and remains an impoverished version of the old."

The point here is to show as forcibly as possible, that the introduction of an anonymous machine – the apparently innocuous clock – brought in its wake mind boggling consequences. It is my thesis that the computer, an even more autonomous device, will in its present form unleash forces that will bring about further dramatic changes in society, human relations and our concept of what it is to be human.

We may be excused for not anticipating some of the outcomes of the clock. It was, after all, the first autonomous machine. But we should learn from that example, and understand that we should devote some thought to the consequences of computerisation before we regret those paths not taken.

It is frequently said that those who don't like computers will simply ignore them and thereby avoid their consequences. This is rather like saying you will live in central London, refuse to have a clock or read clocks, will not listen to the time announcements on the media but nonetheless succeed in participating in London society. It is rather that the technology begins to be a leading edge in those organisations and systems which mould our society, and that society then engulfs the individual. The same may be seen in respect of the printing press, although I hold that although its impact was very great, it pales into insignificance compared with the clock. The printing press and the printed word did, of course, change many aspects of our society, but it wrought those changes even when large sections of the community were incapable of reading, since the printed word transformed the leading sectors in society, which then ultimately transforms society as a whole.

Up to very recently indeed, the majority of people could not read, yet we could not say that the printed word did not dramatically change their lives in a host of manners. Likewise, the fact that large numbers of people do not yet use computers, should not be taken to mean that computerisation, the organisation of forms which surround it, and its anonymous nature will not have dramatic and long reaching effects on our society.

Chapter 11

The Invisible Menders

"The white people never cared for land or deer or bear. When we Indians kill meat, we eat it all up. When we dig roots, we make little holes; we shake down acorns and pinenuts. We don't chop down the trees. We only use dead wood. But the White people plough up the ground, pull up the trees, kill everything. The tree says 'Don't, I am sore. Don't hurt me!'. But they chop it down and cut it up. The spirit of the land hates them. They blast out trees and stir it up to its depths. They saw up the trees. They blast rocks and scatter them on the ground. The rock says, 'Don't! You are hurting me!' But the White people pay no attention. When the Indians use rocks, they take little round ones for their cooking .... How can the spirit of the earth like the White man? ... Everywhere the White man has touched it, it is sore."

Wintu Indian woman

"Put a tiger in your tank"

early 1980s UK advert

What a stark contrast there is in the cultural attitudes to our environment and materials – the gentle animism of some cultures and the crude materialism of our own. In one, the closeness to nature, so close as to see oneself as an integral part of it and in the other, the rapacious alienated consumerism of the industrial societies. We refer to such societies as being materialistic. That is true at one level, but at one level only. At another more significant level, we show contempt for material. We consume it, burn it and dispose of it as though there were no tomorrow. We make exceptions of course. There are, for example, the precious metals. This loaded expression means that other metals are not precious. We have a strange sense of preciousness with regard to special materials – gold, silver, platinum, diamonds. It is not really that we celebrate them or love them and wonder at their composition, colour and form. It is that they have a high exchange value, that they appear to confer status upon us and symbolise our power and wealth.

This is very different from the way a diamond cutter may marvel at the shape of a diamond, understand its crystalline structure, know precisely where to strike it to end up with the most beautiful facets. Nor is it the same as the manner in which a goldsmith can make the material flow under the coaxing of his hammer and ultimately engrave it in both celebration of the material and of his own craft – as indeed, the young Brunelleschi would have done.

This respect for one's material is true not just of diamond cutters and goldsmiths but of all craftspeople. The cobbler or the saddle-maker will not only recognise a fine specimen of leather, but will know that this is part of a wider integrity, namely an animal. These craftsmen will usually know the terrain and circumstances in which that animal grew, the difference between those that developed in the cold hilly highlands and those in the more benign lowlands. They will understand the effect these environments have had on the skins and ultimately, therefore, on the material with which they are working. They will know which part of the resultant material to use for specific parts of the object they are making. The robust, durable material for the sole of a shoe and the supple, almost velvet-like texture for the tongue.

It is a marvel of geometry to watch a saddler cutting out

the forms so as to make best use of the material. Each component is cut out as though it were ultimately part of a whole which, when put together, forms an exquisite jigsaw of the original piece of material. Narrow strips in between, far from being redundant, may turn out to be thongs or straps or retainers for buckles. Everything is carefully used. The sections to be jointed will be perforated with holes of a particular size, spaced so as to provide for the best form of joint – be that rigid or flexible. I have some 'leg o'mutton' cases made over a century ago, whose rich brown leather, brass fittings and hand stitched seams combine in a quality product which is a delight to own and a pleasure to use. Opening its snug fitting leather hinged lid reveals the unselfconscious skill of the craftsmen who designed and made it. It has lasted a 'lifetime' and will last for several more subject only to its material being occasionally 'fed with leather food' whose natural waxes and oils seem to rekindle again and again the beauty of the original and complement it with the patina of a cherished maturing.

Not only are new objects of extraordinary beauty created by the craftsman in leather, but old ones are repaired by techniques involving "invisible mending". Narrow sample strips will be used to experiment with tanning and colouring methods to ensure a superb matching of the old and the new.

In all of these activities, to waste material would be sacreligious to the craftsman. Pieces for which there are no immediate requirements – remnants, as they were sometimes known, or pieces recovered in the course of restoration of older products – would be carefully stored until an opportunity presented itself to make full use of a piece of material which, to the inexperienced may seem merely rubbish. One of the saddest features of modern industrial society is that most people think of all materials as rubbish if they are not fulfilling their short term, specific functionality. The world of the invisible mender is giving way to the reign of the visible destroyer.

The animism of the Wintu Indian is neither possible nor desirable in the industrial societies as we move towards the 21st Century. What is possible, and is of burning necessity, is a new set of values in relation to the environment and materials. As matters stand at the moment, we have a spectrum of concern that ranges from the crude consumeristic vandalism to the caring craft or skill approach. At one end of the spectrum there stands the delinquent, and at the other end the genius of our species. The one unsustainable even in the very short term, and the other desirable and sustainable. Even now, with the ecological disaster looming in front of us, we still rush oblivious towards the siren call of the vandals.

The skilled craft ethos is dangerously weakened by industrial society but not fatally so. There still resides there, the seeds of a tradition still capable of propogation and transplantation to more fertile fields where craft and new technology can combine to provide for a safe, satisfying and creative future.

The craft approach to which I refer was never solely the preserve of 'craftsmen'. It was much more pervasive than we realise. It surfaced frequently in almost all areas of human endeavour. Cooking is but one example. I refer here, not to the great chefs and professional cooks but rather, to ordinary people who were capable of making a creative use of such materials as they had to hand and could, for example, bake ten or fifteen types of bread in their own home, make Christmas puddings, cook and elaborately decorate wedding cakes for their sons and daughters, and make a variety of dishes, producing an astonishing range of flavours from such food that happened to be available. Furthermore, they made great use of it, for no part of the vegetable, the fowl, the fish or the meat would be discarded. Potato skins were fed to fowl; feathers were stored for pillows and matresses; bones, although "picked clean as a whistle" not only delighted waiting dogs but, it was said, sharpened their teeth and 'did their digestion no end of good!' In this we detect the lingering tracks of a more sustainable use of material.

Many of these skills, being ones exercised by women, were not even recognised as skills. Rather they were looked upon as part of being a good housewife or servant. We are all of us, men, women, children, scientists, manual workers, clerks, medical practitioners, mechanics etc., going to have to learn to be good 'housekeepers' if planet Earth is going to survive in a habitable form. For the ultimate house, our ultimate home, is the planet itself.

Dressmaking is another case in point. The skills of fashion designers, royal dressmakers and Savile Row tailors will of course be universally recognised. What is ignored is the reservoir of skills built up by generations of housewives in making clothes for their families. The human body is an odd shape indeed, and there are no two in the whole world which are precisely the same in a scientific sense. To produce the garment which fits it well is no mean task as many computer scientists are now finding out as they seek to produce computer aided design systems for the garment industry. As a result, there are standardised sizes, one of which we expect to fit into. Like most members of the public, I can't afford to have suits tailor-made. I don't ask to be measured and attend for a 'fitting', I just look along the racks for a specific chest, waist and leg length which is most likely to pass as a fit. There is usually a dazzling range of shortlife "close to form components" to chose from.

However, not only were bygone housewives able to make clothes for the family, they were also capable of the even greater task of recycling existing garments. How many wedding dresses blossomed anew as evening wear or confirmation attire for daughters? How many men's suits were revitalised to surface, devoid of the frayed cuffs, shiny seats and worn out elbows, as school gear for young sons? One simply did not waste a "nice piece of cloth" because it had outlived its immediate functionality. I can still recall myself, families in which a good piece of material formed the basis of a cascade of use as it travelled through the family. There was too another recycling of good materials when parents produced garments for school plays, festive dress for carnivals, outfits for dolls and for dressing up. Knitted garments would be unravelled and reconstituted in some new form. Many a summer dress metamorphised into a pinafore, a pillow case or sections of a multicoloured patchwork quilt. Those capable of doing such creative recycling, correctly felt a sense of pride and achievement as a result.

What was vital about this was a sense that one did not discard good material. One cherished, celebrated and re-used it. In addition to a craft respect for the material and the imagination to plan and envisage its resurrection, this was frequently driven by sheer economic necessity. Now an even more compelling necessity bears in on us; that of the preservation of our planet.

Technology has come between us and our materials to such an extent that we can no longer cherish, respect or even recognise them. The arm of a suit shown on the screen of a Computer Aided Design system, conveys none of the feel of a fine tweed. Even the most powerful graphic systems, when they display the leg of a chair under design consideration, can say virtually nothing at the subjective level, of the weight, surface texture or beautiful grain of a fine piece of wood. That can and does only come from working on the material by hand. This will require a balance between hand and brain. Our hand is as much a part of us as our brain, and using it requires effort of a different kind, but no less significant than the effort involved in using our brain. Both contribute to our essence and our consciousness and for me, the hand has always been the leading edge of the brain. Orwell put it with startling frankness:

> "Above the level of a third or fourth grade moron, life has got to be lived largely in terms of effort ... Cease to use your hands and you have lobbed off a huge chunk of your consciousness."

One of the great challenges facing society will be to devise means of production, design product ranges and organise work processes so as to retain and enhance that consciousness, that same closeness to materials, whilst minimising that part of work which was backbreaking or soul destroying; for some areas of manual skill were very double edged indeed.

Woodworking of all kinds provides for this deep sense of the material. That is true if we are talking about the finest forms of cabinet making, or that work which outwardly appears comparatively simple and physical, but inwardly involve all kinds of skill and knowledge. Seldom have craftsmen written about their skills since skill was transmitted, not in the written word but in the muscular and nervous system of the craftsmen themselves and their apprentices. "Written", as James Joyce put it, though in a different context "on the only foolscap available – his own body".

There were exceptions. George Sturt, in his book *The Wheelwright's Shop*, shows a fine combination of the gifts of a craftsman and the powers of a writer and has given us a vivid account of the hard graft and the skill that combines to provide for the whole activity of wheelwrights. He describes work which has not yet reached that fragmentation, subdivision and separation that Schiller feared when he predicted that we would reach a stage when:

> "Enjoyment is separated from labour, the means from the end, exertion from compensation. Eternally fettered only to a single little fragment of the whole, man fashions himself only as a fragment, ever hearing only the monotonous whirl of the wheel which he turns, he never develops the harmony of his being and instead of shaping the humanity that lies in his nature, he becomes a mere imprint of his occupation, his science."

Sturt describes the journeys to select the timber from the forests and his capacity to understand the enormous difference between 'winter-cut' and 'spring-cut' oak. He could analyse a wide range of material because:

> "my own eyes know because my hands have felt, but I cannot teach an outsider the difference between ash that is tough as whipcord and ash that is frow as a carrot or doaty or biscuity."

He brings to life for his readers the skill and toil of the sawyers working in a sawpit. He describes the means by which the tree is located over the sawpit and the techniques used by the sawyers to ensure the optimum number of boards from a given tree.

As the work commences, he tells us of the fascination in watching the ever lengthening parallel cuts down the tree:

"to see them growing, growing quarter inch, nothing shirking (every speck of sawdust had to be cut out) yet so relentlessly. Oh it was like watching fate at work. There is no need to picture the 'mills of God' to anybody who has ever seen sawyers converting a big elm tree into boards."

One can still marvel at the co-ordination of physical effort of the sawyers with their huge crosscuts and their precision in cutting one inch planks the entire length of the tree to tolerances of parallelsim which were a tribute to hand and brain. But related to this was the terrible hard graft which gave rise to the picturesque description of an unfortunate person as being "always bottom sawyer".

The bottom sawyer worked in the pit below the tree – often in stifling heat for hour after hour. There is nothing romantic or Utopian about this kind of work. As Sturt puts it: "Laborious it was in the extreme, and the sawdust poured down on his sweating face and bare arms and down his back". But this was merely a gruelling prelude to the marvellously skilled work that would follow, on a material that was cherished for the labour that had already gone into it. He describes the making of the dish wheels, forming the spokes which go into them and the tacit techniques involved. Bookish training was too feeble to enter into these final secrets. Evidently, there was something more only revealed to the skilled hands and eyes after years of experience .

Sturt emphasises the care taken in selecting the most appropriate wood for the spokes, and then the use of "a more delicate tool significantly called the spokeshave". Those who have seen the wheels of such coaches at South Kensington museum or at country fairs, still marvel at the elegance of the shape and the appropriateness to task. He describes the rejection of the early machine-made "commodities originating from America, heavy and clumsy finished, even to my eyes but they seem to offend George Cook still more and save for an emergency, he unwillingly used them. He was too much an artist in spokes".

So even down to the smallest detail there was artistry. This highlights a major point I wish to make. There was a deep sense of the "effort" the tree had made in growing the wood, of the laborious task of preparing it into the rough blanks as a prelude to the fine shaping of the desired object – the wheel. But the relationship with the wheel didn't end there. Even as the wheel wore it would be sacreligious to throw away such beautiful material. So he tells us that after thirty years or so, the spokes would still be sound and were taken out carefully. "I sold thousands of them at a penny a piece for ladder rungs, but the better of them were set aside to be worked up again as smaller spokes for barrow wheels. Then they might start another career of usefulness for another twenty or thirty years."

The whole process now seems light years away from the Saturday morning shopper who drives to the local furniture emporium to select a piece to grace their home for a brief interval on its way to the nearest Council tip. Indeed, it often seems that such items were designed more for the tip than for the home.

In contrast, what shines through in the accounts of craftsman's work is a deep sense of the material. I recall highly skilled carpenters making doors for which they would select the wood so that each panel had a matching "knot" to create a symmetrical form. But more particularly, I remember that they would hang the door, and then return with their tools some six months later to finally fit it into position when, as they put it, "the wood had settled down". It was almost as though they were talking about the inhabitants themselves settling into a new home. When finally fitted, such doors closed snugly into their frames with a smooth 'clonk' which resonated quality of material and craftsmanship. The doors were made to last for years and years and years – and they did.

We may observe that the craftsman worked with the material rather than against it. Building on its strengths and minimising its weaknesses. All craftspeople are aware of this need, and from this, we characterise an abrasive or unsatisfactory situation in a wider context as one where something "goes against the grain". All cultures traditionally embody this respect for materials. In Japanese, the tools for carpentry are referred to as *dogu*. This has no real equivalent in any other language. It means roughly "the instruments of the way" – the way of doing carpentry. It is no pun to say that in modern society we have lost our way. I have dealt with these issues in considerable detail, because I wish to propose that we have to look into the past to perceive the future.

I have suggested in a recent major FAST Report that we now need a Cultural and Industrial Renaissance in Europe. In such a renaissance, we will reunite our sense of material and craft skill with new technologies in such a way as to develop sustainable forms of products and means of producing them. This would restore to us our sense of feeling for materials and for skill, but will avoid that backbreaking form of labour represented by the bottom sawyer in the sawpit. Roger Coleman catches this sense of what is necessary when he tells us:

"We talk about a feeling for wood or stone, which the machine does not have, a flair for cooking, the green fingers of the gardener and so on, all ideas which suggest something far removed from the subject-object relationships of our autocratic technologies. We dispense drugs and fertilizers by pushing buttons, and become increasingly distanced from the materials and techniques we use.

But a physical sensitivity to the materials of a trade or craft is central to skill itself, distinguishing the traditional, sympathetic arts from dispassionate modern manufacturing processes, and it is this very sensitivity, a sensitivity which has taken generations to develop, that we are on the verge of losing.

By reviving this traditional use of the word art we can recognise that art and skill are, or were, identical. Cookery is an art, we still call it that, so is fishing, and from this point of view all the sensitive, symbiotic traditional skills are arts. The joiner is an artist in wood. We still use expressions like this, and the ideas lie dormant in our language. Nor is this sort of art a strange, inscrutable activity, but the very way in which skills are used and practised, with art and artistry. Indeed, until very recently it would have been perfectly correct to describe as arts all those skills learned by apprenticeship and by practice.

As a definition, this usage is much closer to the original meaning of the word art. People who make things well are artists, and vice versa, and it is this doing and making things well, with care and concern for how and why they are made, that brings real quality into everyday life. As a definition, it accounts for both the 'fine' and the 'useful' arts equally well, for both are ways of doing things well, and therefore of bringing quality into everyday life, a quality which takes us beyond material wealth, and gives us a truer way of measuring value than a market economy does."

None of this should be taken as some kind of romantic harping back to the past, but rather as a vital development if our society is going to be able to sustain itself. Many of the underlying ideas were prefigured in the sixteen definitions of socially useful production developed by the Lucas workers in the mid 70's and set out in *Architect or Bee?* Now, centres throughout Europe are seriously considering these issues at the level of basic design itself. It questions that productionist notion of mass producing products which are nothing more than the functions they perform. When the product ceases to function, or worse still, when it simply falls out of fashion, it is disposed of. There is no sense in which it is understood that this product is far more than its functionality implies. It has embodied within it materials which could be used for other purposes, just as the spokes were in the wheelwright's workshop.

As we design objects in future, we have to bear this new dimension in mind. At the first level, we should design products in such a form as to render them easily repairable, with deliberately built in longevity. Every time we throw away a product, we are throwing away an equivalent amount of energy. The frantic drive for more energy leads to the Greenhouse Effect, demands for more nuclear power stations and ultimate damage to the environment.

Over and above this, we should so design products that at the end of their long and extended life, their materials can then be extracted and used in different forms. In the past, when a table ceased to be a table skilled carpenters would always use the legs or the boards for other articles. Professor Manzini, director of the Design Division at the Domas Academy in Milan points out:

"What about the world that you have to take care of, and no longer a world of things that you discard. Objects that last and hence objects that require maintenance, may seem at first like

130

an added burden, but think about gardens. People keep gardens for the fruit and vegetables the garden gives, or the beauty of the flowers but at least in part, they have gardens in order to take care of them."

In large numbers we have lost the capacity to care and are careless in a tragically irresponsible way.

Manzini suggests new forms of products in which we inbuild at the design stage a capacity to age well, a patina of age that develops giving the ageing product new qualities. We all of us, at some stage in our lives, however dehumanised we are by new technologies, have enjoyed looking after some objects which we treasure. Who, at some stage or another hasn't felt the thrill of acquiring some object, purchased perhaps at a jumble sale, say an antique, an old clock or a damaged article and breathing life back into it again. The future will require people capable of doing this on a grand scale. People who have the hands of a craftsperson, the heart of an ecologist and the mind of a scientist. We can even embark upon the research task of developing materials which would display the kind of characteristics I have indicated above – that as they age, they display new characteristics and qualities which are wholesome and desirable.

These new concepts we can and should extend to all products. This will involve a new cultural outlook, a new respect for materials, for the environment and therefore for ourselves. As a crude generalisation, we may say that people today manifest their wellbeing and status by the amount of energy and materials they squander, whether that be by jetsetting round the world, possessing and driving numerous gas guzzling cars, overheating their several homes, and throwing away their various possessions as whim and fashion dictate. We shall have to move to a more frugal and caring society in which wastage of materials will be seen as the essence of bad taste; where the wasting of energy and materials will be culturally and socially as unacceptable as defecating on one's doorstep.

Such changes can only come when people are aware of what it is they are doing. The question of awareness is of key importance. In the past, if one had to collect wood for the fire, saw up and then split the logs, one had some direct sense of the amount of material required to produce a certain level of warmth. Technology, and the marketing systems which support it, separate us from the use of materials or render that use less visible.

The point may be illustrated by considering that symbol of mass production – the car. In most of the technologically advanced nations, we either own a car or at least travel occasionally in one owned by somebody else. When in cities we spend a lot of our time dodging them to ensure we are not knocked down. They cram our car parks and motorways and are parked outside our houses.

Yet in spite of this intimate relation between human beings in industrial societies and their cars, we really have little idea of their wider impact or the energy they use. We even find it difficult to conceptualise the impact they have on our health. According to the American Lung Association, ground level Ozone smog is caused mainly by car emissions, and poses the most serious health problem in the United States. Estimates of the increased health care costs of disease caused by air pollution put it at one dollar for each gallon of fuel used in a car or $133.8 billion annually in the USA alone.

Ninety per cent of all the air pollution in cities and thirty per cent of the greenhouse gases come from fossil fuelled transport. Burning one gallon of petroleum yields twenty two pounds weight of Carbon Dioxide, the major greenhouse gas. But how many of us can really conceptualise what this means? We might do so if we took forty four half pound packets of butter (each roughly 500g) and stacked them on top of each other. That is the weight of carbon dioxide each gallon of petrol yields. We now begin to get some slight sense of what is going on. If, in a combination of city, urban and rural driving, our average car does twenty-seven miles to the gallon, then in the expected lifetime of that car it will emit thirty-seven tons of carbon dioxide or about thirty seven times the weight of the car itself!

If we realised this as distinct from just knowing it, we would behave differently. One could go on to point out that if the car is thrown away when it has done eighty thousand miles or ten years old, the energy it has required to drive it is still only about equal to the energy used to produce it in the first place. Yet we design cars to fall apart after four or five years. More outrageously, we look at those parts of the world where the number of cars is significantly smaller than our own scandalous figures and see it as "an underdeveloped market". The assumption is that a similar density of car usage can ultimately be achieved in those areas.

We urgently need to rethink all of this, and in the interim design alternatives to the existing vehicle types. Electrical vehicles for example, although not without their own forms of problems, do show major reductions in toxic emissions. It has been estimated that if just one per cent of the cars in the United States were electric, emissions would be cut by a hundred thousand tons a year and sixty thousand barrels of oil a day would be saved. If such vehicles were partly solar powered, and so designed as to be repairable and of long life, then improvements in the short term could be made. The possibility of gaseous hydrogen fuel cells for cars could likewise be explored.

What is vital, however, is that there is a consumer culture and a design culture which looks at ways of organising our use of materials and products such as to ensure the minimum man made, environmental impact. From a technical point of view it is relatively easy to design vehicles that will last very much longer and be repairable, but all of this requires on the part of designers, users and society, a relationship to the product which more closely resembles that of the craft tradition explained above.

I have chosen the car because it is a familiar example. Clearly, one has to think in the wider context of much better, safer, lower environmental impact public transport systems, but also beyond transport, the way we use materials and relate to products as a whole will have to dramatically change before it is too late.

We shall have to use great ingenuity to succeed with this challenge before it is too late. The genius of our species must assert itself before the delinquent does irreversible damage. I have described elsewhere the task which now confronts us as that of a cultural and industrial renaissance. My colleague Tony Fry sees the task no less urgent in the context of what he calls 'Sacred Design'. He reflects on the question posed by Heidegger: "Do we stand in the very twilight of the most monstrous transformation our planet has ever undergone, the twilight of that epoch in which earth itself hangs suspended? Do we confront the evening with the light of another dawn? Are we to strike off on a journey to this historic region of the earth's evening?" Tony replies: "For the love of life, there is but one answer to each of Heidegger's questions. We must shout yes!"

"What follows from this affirmation then, is that we have eminently the act of creation as re-creation before us. Increasingly, it is being realised in science and society that if we, humanity, continue to damage the life of the global organism upon which we depend in the ways that we have done so far, then our destruction is assured. To put it bluntly, and acknowledging the difference of our life roles, no matter what deflections call, divert or console, if we want to survive we have to face the fact that the act of our own re-creation is before us by necessity."

He continues:

"The sacred I seek to expose, as non scientific theory of design is profoundly profane. It is of the earth and the elements. It makes no appeal to spirit beyond us. Rather it posits faith in the celebration and action of a common love of life which brought us to social being and ever drives us towards survival. It is faith we have to find/create in the world of objects."

CHAPTER 12

SPECTATOR STATUS

Hurling is an ancient Gaelic game. It has been an obsession with Celtic peoples back into the mists of time. Mythology has it that it was the favourite sport of the Great Mythical Figure Cuchullin (The Hound of Cullin). As the young man Setanta, he was brought up in the court of King Connach. On one occasion when the king and his noblemen were going to a feast at the Doon of Cullin, Setanta, who was to go with them, was so engrossed in his game of Hurling that he asked the King to go ahead and said he would follow later. It was said that Cuchullin was so swift of foot that he could hit a hurling ball into the air at a low trajectory and run ahead and catch it. Even if this was unlikely, it was certainly impressive imagery. When eventually Cuchullin had completed his game, and then set off after the King, the postponement created by his obsession led to the renaming of Setanta as Cuchullin, the greatest of all the Celtic Warriors.

Having been delayed by his game of Hurling, he proceeded on to the Down of Cullin. By then it was getting dark and Cullin, as was his practice each night, had set on guard outside his house a huge and ferocious dog. The dog attacked the unsuspecting Setanta and in the fierce battle that followed, the young boy slayed the dog to the amazement of the warriors, the King and Cullin himself when they finally arrived at the scene. Setanta pledged himself to guard

Cullin's home until he had found a new guard dog, and as a commemoration of his first deed of valour, they named him Cuchullin.

The obsession with Hurling remains with many young Celtic people to this very day, even if its forms and outcomes are less dramatic. It is played on a football-size pitch with two teams of 15 each side. They play with a hurley with which they hit a leather ball towards the goal on the opposing side. It is a fast moving game as the ball can be driven from one end of the pitch to the other in a very short length of time. It looks quite ferocious as the opposing sides clash in a "rush" with hurleys swinging and the ball, no bigger than a cricket ball, emerging to shoot with astonishing velocity three quarters of the way along the pitch. It is said that the German Ambassador in Dublin in the '30s remarked when watching the game that if the Irish played like that, he wondered what they would be like in war.

Actually the game is very skilful and surprisingly few injuries are sustained, even when compared with other field games. To this day, I marvel at the skill, timing and ease with which a skilled performer can intercept the ball in flight with a hurley and redirect it from one flightpath to another more desired one with the deft flick of a wrist. It would be a complicated task to work it all out mathematically and study the mechanics of the different techniques used. We acquire them easily and naturally by watching and emulating other skilled performers such as the senior boys at school or even some of the County Champions who, on occasion, would deign to give a 7 or 8 year old a precious tip as to how this or that might be done. By the time we were 10 or 11, we regarded ourselves as highly proficient in the art.

We had also acquired some of the related skills such as selecting a Hurley. We knew that the grain should follow the curve of the enlarged end so that as it impacted the ball or another hurley stick, it was much less likely to fracture. We would test its flexibility by holding one end in our hand, the other end against the ground, and with the second hand press on it about one third of the way up to see that it flexed well and sprang back nicely. This would ensure that in precarious moments it was resilient enough to absorb the impact of another hurley stick, and was not too rigid and inclined to shatter. Actually, rather like people have to be able to absorb the shock and blows that life so often delivers.

Like all human activities, it was performed within a culture, within a context of skills, attributes and above all, a social context. It wasn't just the skills of the game or the subtle competitive aspects but the social context in which it took place. It was even possible, through these activities, to get an early inkling at the age of 9 of what we might refer to now as sexual politics. Boys played hurling and Girls played Camogie. The games were the same in every essential respect – the same Hurley sticks, the same size ball, the same length of pitch, the same numbers of players – just a different name.

My sister Mabel was a talented Comogie player who subsequently captained the county team. Even at that early stage she was a formidable player. She would frequently play midfield and if she did so with her trusted team mate, the skilful and fiery Rosy McDonagh, they were a midfield duo that required some stopping. When the 'roadteams' were practising and finding it difficult to muster the full 30 to cover all positions, they would reluctantly allow a couple of the girls to play for our side, but only for practice of course. In these depleted circumstances, Mabel would play full forward. That meant that she would mark the opposition's full back Seamus. The truth was she could play rings around him. When she did so, he would complain under his breath to the half back that she was lucky to be always in the right place at the right time. Had it been a male colleague it might have had something to do with brilliant fieldwork. When he would go for the ball believing he had outpaced her and she came up behind him just as he was about to strike, this was seen disparagingly as sly and cunning playing, rather than good field tactics.

At the end of the match, Seamus would leave the field exhausted, confused and, despite his most strenuous efforts, completely outplayed. He would confide to his team-mates in low tones and with typical male blustering, that she was lucky she was just a girl or he would have played with his full force and made smitherines of her. Gradually through our play, there would unfold for us all the subtleties, complexities, delights, deviousness, and disappointments of life in general. It was a marvellous education!

There were about five major roads which emanated spoke-like from the town square. Every road had its own hurling team and there was ferocious rivalry between them. Each year there was an unofficial, informal but fiercely contested road league. Before you ever got near the playing field you had to define 'a road'. There were convoluted and complex negotiations as to what constituted a road. It was extraordinary how far out into the countryside a road would go, or so argued its team, if there happened to be a formidable player at the end of it. Then there were the small crossroads in between, and 10 year olds would argue long and with great eloquence whether one could allocate half the length of the cross road to each team instead of those on either side of the road.

The unwritten agenda of all these negotiations was to

define 'a road' so as to justify the good players being in ones own road team, and the plodders on the other side. We learned that definitions were seldom absolute and can be notorious traps for the unwary! All this intensity, coping, defining and negotiating is only possible when you are involved – deeply involved – in a process.

These were but the preliminary machinations as a prelude to the event itself, the game. As the day approached there would be rumours that a representative (always unnamed) of one team had offered a fishing reel to the lead player of another to feel unwell on the great day. One's own team was of course completely above such corrupt practices! Teams would develop their tactics in secrecy and often through the mediation of parents, uncles, cousins, relatives or assorted acquaintances. A competent senior hurler might be recruited to give special tips at secret practice sessions. Some of the manouverings of these 10 and 11 year olds make modern executive business games look like what confused adults (and in particular educationalists) dismissively call 'child's play'.

The selection of the teams to play each other was also part of the deadly earnest power game. Ideally, one should meet a weak team in the first round and play them on their home ground so that at the more difficult stage, one would be playing 'on home ground'. This was a euphemism for some field close to the road in question. The flatness of the pitch and the length of the grass were all vital to knowing how to play on it to full advantage in different circumstances.

Only the final game would be played in the 'real pitch' which had goalposts and a crossbar. In all the critical eliminating matches, the goal was improvised by having two bundles of coats marking its width. This provided great latitude for interpretation, argument, and even the odd bit of sleight of hand. Some teams even stooped so low as to gradually move the coats closer together so the width of the goal gradually diminished as the match went on. This of course was crucial, for if a ball rolled along the ground between the two bundles, it was a goal. If, however, the ball rolled onto or over a bundle, there was of course a basis for considerable dispute, and the next generation of solicitors, politicians and other dubious professions, could be detected in embryo amongst the 10 year olds. In arguing whether it was a goal or not a goal, they would reach considerable heights of eloquence, plausibility or sheer argumentation. Some of them, it was said, had the ability "to talk the cross off a donkey's back", and all of this was when the ball ran on the ground! In the air, the ambiguity was several orders of magnitude greater. Did the ball pass over the bundle of coats or not? Was it merely that you were standing in a certain position and therefore it *appeared* to cross over the bundle of coats, but did not do so.

When playing on the *real* pitch, if the ball went between the goalposts but under the crossbar that was a goal! If it went between the posts but over the crossbar, that was a point. Since in the preliminary games there were no goal posts, much less crossbars, the scope for judgement, logic, interpretation and downright cheating was considerable, but what a marvellous preparation for life it was!

The final for the street league was normally played in July. The match would run from about 7.30 to 9.30. If you won the toss and the sky was not cloudy, you would make sure that your opponents had to play against the sun. By the time the second half came, with luck it would be behind or at least partly concealed by the trees. The final that year was once again our road, Tullinadaly Road against Ballygaddy

Road. We had long since dispensed with Dublin Road, Bishop Sreet and the Galway Road.

The year before, my aunt in Galway had given me a great pair of football boots. They were ideal for Hurling, gave me a good solid grip on the ground and allowed me to accelerate and decelerate better than shoes lacking seggs. As the spring wore on and we were eliminating the opposition road teams, the boots began to pinch more and more for a 10 year old grows rapidly at that time. I refused to admit that they were really pinching my feet, even though they began to be quite painful and as the spring merged into summer, my toe was increasingly painful, until there was the awful discovery three weeks before the match that I had a serious ingrown toe nail.

A plethora of useless remedies were tried and found wanting. Some verged on the surgical, such as cutting a small V in the top of the nail, which I had been assured would cause the nail to converge towards the centre, thereby relieving pressure on the offending side. But it was all to no avail and four days prior to the match, I had to admit that I could not play.

The team agreed that Michael Moroney should take my place. He was a good player but of course when you're 10 years old, nobody plays as good as you do. I used to play full back and coached him on all the potential pitfalls of that role. I told him which members of the opposition team to look out for and to take particular care of Gabriel Heskin and Noel Loftus. Secretly I suppose I hoped he wouldn't play all that well, and indeed if we lost the match, it might be said we lost because I was not able to play. Such are the contradictions between collective and personal loyalties, but on balance, I dearly wanted my team to win and coached him earnestly for that outcome. On that Thursday evening,

I still recall limping up to watch the match. Last minute advice was given if not always taken and the match commenced.

It was the first time that I had been a spectator in those circumstances. It wasn't like being a spectator at a match when two other teams were playing. Here I was a spectator as my own team played. Part of me was out there yet I was now detached from that which helped make me what I was. The sense of exclusion and helplessness was intense. There was a tree at the corner of the field close to the fullback's position. It had a well distributed range of branches not all that far apart and was really quite easy to climb, even with my throbbing toenail. I had done it many, many times before but now I was doing it so that I could better observe the subtelty and progress of the match. I got to the top of the tree and had a birdseye view of the pitch in a very real sense for often a grey crow would perch there. I could see all parts of the field and I was close enough to be able to shout advice to Michael Moroney.

I could see right down the far end of the field when the opposition team were preparing for an onslaught. I could see the positioning of each of their players and could almost see in advance what it was they were going to do. I would shout endless instructions to Michael Moroney – "Look out!", "take care!", "watch Gabriel Heskin", "Loftus is dribbling the ball up along the lefthand side".

No matter how clear my instructions however, it did not seem to avail of any significant outcome. Michael Moroney's view would be obscured by the players in front of him. There would be a rush and suddenly the ball would shoot forward as he confided in me afterwards, "like a bat out of hell". What a strange combination of biological, aerodynamic and punitive religious imagery all at once, but I knew exactly what he meant as did every other player who has suddenly been confronted with a ball hurtling towards them at 20 or 30 miles per hour when on the wrong foot and your hurly held in the wrong position.

He played well, very well, but my perspective from my higher perch was not *his* perspective. He was on the ground. He was amongst it all and it was what he saw and did that determined the outcome and not my perspective from my frustrating spectator position.

That event brought home to me in simple but dynamic terms the difference between a participant and a spectator. Modern life is turning more and more of us into spectators. Indeed we are doing it ourselves voluntarily! At least I was driven to it in that event by an ingrown toenail. Now we are driven to it by ingrown minds! We now spectate whilst others (or machines) cook, others make clothes, or even sing. In the past we all of us used to sing except those afflicted (as they used to put it) with "no ear for music". Now how many of us sing or even have the desire to do so? Our spectator status has been gradually emerging, discernably so over the last 500 years. Let us see how and why we so diminish ourselves.

* * *

The instinct to participate is deeply rooted in our species. We live through participation. A simple, but good description of death is that point at which we cease to participate.

The transition to death – old age – is a process in which the active human being is gradually transformed into spectator. There is a graceful degradation but however graceful, it is nonetheless a degradation. The old person doesn't drive the car any more, but as passenger, sits alongside somebody who does. He doesn't play football any more, just watches football games on television. She doesn't garden any more but, if wealthy enough, will get somebody to garden for her. Facilities and capabilities gradually drop off like petals from an autumn rose. Eventually they are: "sans teeth, sans eyes, sans taste, sans everything". It is a natural biological process. Growing old is just as natural as growing up.

That reality is an obvious biological and acceptable one at the individual level. The elderly take comfort and often pleasure in the fact that later generations of participants are following them who are full of life and energy. The assumption is that society invigorates itself by a continuous infusion of youth participants, always growing and developing. If, however, we develop our technology and organise our society in such a way that at an earlier and earlier stage we behave as spectators, then we may see whole cultures and large sections of our species in decline. Instead of encouraging the youth of our species to continuously replace, replenish and revitalise society, we may observe that we are conferring that evolutionary responsibility on machines. In doing so, we are ushering in the old age of our species as a whole. Whereas in the past we looked to the next generation to provide youth, energy and vitally active participation, we now confer those attributes and evolutionary elements on machines and confer old age on ourselves.

Strangely, although we accept the inevitability of old age at an individual biological level, we do nonetheless in general refuse into go gently to that dark night, and we recognise:

> "How dull it is to pause, to make an end, to rust unburnished not to shine in use".

We seem now to have gradually moved towards a stage where the species as a whole will cease to shine in use. Partly, this is due to our own 'cleverness'.

Somebody recently pointed out to me that it is extremely dangerous to be clever if one lacks wisdom. We are now far too clever to be able to survive long without wisdom. Part of our cleverness has been to devise machines, systems and processes as a means of getting rid of the hard, messy, difficult aspects of life and thereby freeing ourselves to deal only with the 'challenging activities'. This way of looking at things ignores how challenging and profound ordinary activities may be, and how formative and necessary they are for us. So we evolve systems which eliminate much of the messy part of activities and appear to leave the really decisive parts for human intervention.

Computer games are a case in point. It certainly would be possible with modern advanced computer techniques and graphics to produce very powerful simulations of playing hurling. Like other computer games, they would require considerable skill to play and practise and technique would become important. It would however be a very different form of skill. It would be extremely narrow and abstracted. We could ignore the weather when we played it. We could play in the middle of the night when there is no light or in the winter when there is two feet of snow on the ground. The real game would not allow for that. We could avoid the messiness of having to travel to a pitch, arrange for colleagues to be there, negotiate who or what constituted a team and worry about the surface of the pitch.

In avoiding all that, we would of course avoid the rich social context, the communications, the negotiations, the bluffing and the sheer breadth of social and sensory feedback. No vibration would ripple through our muscular and nervous system as the hurley stick impacted the ball and drove it on its hopefully goal-winning trajectory. The angle at which we struck the ball, the sense of the force with which we did it would not flow through that marvellous information gathering system the human body, and store it in that amazing reservoir of ability, the human mind, there to incorporate it in its treasure trove of knowledge to be drawn out at astonishing speed in some analagous situation. But the computer game, pathetic and almost irrelevant substitute that it is, nonetheless shows that we have not entirely extinguished the desire 'to play.'

The desire to participate is reflected at many levels, even in a distorted form. The whole 'do it yourself' DIY syndrome is an attempt to hold on to a part of ourselves which deep down we know to be precious but which we are losing. Very, very few people indeed are now capable of undertaking woodwork in the skilled, historical sense (with rare exceptions to the point of being like threatened species). We have few people who can produce beautiful carved pulpits or delicately fashioned dining tables. Indeed we have very few people who can any longer make dovetailed joints or produce mortise and tenons. Apart from the loss of skills, there no longer exists the special tools, the myriad of chisel choices, the hand held planes with subtle profiles evolved through hundreds of years to produce an astonishing variety of forms and shapes.

There are very few people who can even plane a long

piece of wood so that it is reasonably flat on one surface and is at right angles to another. We do of course like to pretend that we can do all these things. Not only do them indeed, but do them better than they were done at earlier stages. And so there are the specialist shops which facilitate our delusions. One company which produces modular units of wooden kitchen furniture even has a 'design studio'. There, the customer now believing themselves to be a 'designer' can use computer graphics or scale models to "design and make your own kitchen". They have a significant range of choice possibilities so long, of course, as they adhere to the menu, the set number of pieces and range of shapes. With this adult lego set, they can produce either on the screen or in model form, the design of their own kitchen. The company will have it delivered to them as a flat pack which they can screw together and fit to the wall. They can then disclose to their friends that this is the kitchen they have designed and built themselves. The visitor, no doubt equally deskilled, will coo in appropriate admiration.

One should not be too disparaging about this. It is after all, an attempt to be creative, an attempt to be involved in a creative process. But what a poor substitute it is for the real thing!

* * *

The dichotomy between wishing to participate in creative activities and at the same time be a spectator, provides huge markets in a number of ways. Cooking is a case in point. One has only got to go to any reasonable sized bookshop to see the vast array of books on cooking which are on offer. There are books on Italian cooking, Indian cooking, Chinese cooking; books on game cookery, desserts, pastries – the choice is truly baffling.

If one adheres closely to the formula type cooking described in the book, very laudable results can be achieved in terms of the resultant meal. This, though, is not really the point we are making here. In such cook books the ingredients required are prescribed precisely in advance. Some allow a tiny latitude for initiative and we may be informed that we can "add salt to taste". This will be the only quantity that has not been prescribed quite precisely in advance. The amount of meat will have been prescribed. It will state clearly from which part of the animal it should come and whether it should be lean or fat.

In very few cases will the potential cook actually understand the anatomy and structure of the donor animal and it is more a question of asking the butcher or looking at the lists for a piece of the prescribed form. There is no question of being able to prepare the meat oneself. Even where birds or small animals are used in their entirety they still have to be provided in their prepared form. How many cooks, for example, would now know how to pluck and draw a pheasant or even a chicken? How many would be able to clean and skin a rabbit or a hare?

More to the point perhaps, we are no longer really able to take advantage of what happens to be available and improvise a meal around it. We are less able to respond to what nature or our environment has on offer. Berries and fruits available in the wild are ignored by people who purchase them by the pound in the supermarket. Even in urban areas the fruit from laden apple trees will be left to rot rather than be used for cider, chutney or just stewed and frozen for desserts. Most people can't make jam, the simplest way to use excess fruit.

We seek, rather, to impose our predetermined requirements on the environment as well as on ourselves so that we can be passive rather than active in the preparation of the required ingredients for the meal. For example, we are in the process of changing breeding practices so that we produce chickens in a standard meal size e.g. for four persons, and rear animals so that the joints are suitable for what we require at the modern table.

What a difference in background knowledge and competence there now is between the customer who goes to the supermarket and 'selects' a packet of sliced back bacon and farming communities in the past where each family would purchase a pig for slaughter.

This practice was widespread throughout Europe and continues in some remote areas even to this day. Each and every part of the pig will be prepared for use. The blood will be used for black pudding. The less desirable parts – head and trotters – may be used to make 'brawn'. Above all, large sections of it will have to be cured in various ways either by salting or by smoking. Furthermore, the consumption has to be planned in accordance with the means of storage possible and dishes worked out accordingly.

This example may seem grotesque to some readers who, nonetheless, do not find at all contradictory the fact that they will have something similar done to the pig on their behalf in a highly mechanised abbatoir. Our spectator status has become so remote and so distant that it is gradually fading out of our vision, obscured in the abstraction of the abattoir and the pre-packaged product on the shop shelf.

In this high level of abstraction, large numbers of us no longer even realise where the product is coming from. For example, the young daughter of one of my colleagues was horrified to learn that pork sausages came from minced pig, and although she had been an avid eater of grilled sausages for several years, she was incapable of eating them any longer when she learned of their true origin. This could be seen as simply providing a good case for vegetarianism, but how many vegetarians actually understand where the vegetables really come from? I understand from my local garden centre that even when people grow their own vegetables, fewer and fewer members of the public wish to buy seeds and so be involved in the process of growing as far back as possible. Rather they wish to purchase plants already past that precarious and messy stage.

Underlying these issues is what I would describe as a 'state of mind': a spectator state of mind. Even in human reproduction itself we see similar underlying tendencies. A researcher who is a world authority in his field, was recently talking about the development of artificial placentcae and the possibility of couples having children without all the messiness and involvement of a pregnancy. Indeed, he went so far as to suggest that this form of scientific development would ultimately "free women from their biological imperative". The couple would be spectators to the growth of the embryo rather than be participants.

It seems highly desirable to try and trace how this spectator state of mind has come about and to see if it is not possible to so organise our science, technology and society to make the best use of our capabilities whilst still continuing to develop as a species.

CHAPTER 13

THE WINDOW OF DISASTER

Fifteenth Century Florence holds a riveting fascination for me. The city is one of the cradles of our civilisation. Within its walls have sprung to life many of the artefacts and concepts which constitute that which is best in our European civilisation.

Each year, hundreds of thousands of visitors from all over the world arrive in Florence to pay homage to its greatness. It is good that it should be so, and few sensitive visitors will leave without feeling their spirits elevated by the beauty, artistry and symbols of our civilisation which surround them. It is seen as being a wholly positive contribution to our European development and that is perhaps not surprising, but there was another side to this which laid the basis for seriously distorting tendencies in our development.

The centre of the city is Santa Maria del Fiore. Rising majestically above the city from the cruciformed shape of the church is the Cupola which was designed and built by Filippo Brunelleschi. Even by present day standards the dome, which is one of the biggest in Christendom, is a structure of astonishing size and mind boggling complexity. Professors at the University of Florence are using very advanced computing systems with the latest graphic techniques to try and obtain a better understanding of the structural elements of the Cupola, yet it was designed and built in the 15th century. This was a time in European culture when, for the first time, the word "design" began to emerge in most of the European languages.

The emergence of the word did not connotate a new activity "designing", but rather was suggesting that the design activity was being separated out of the wider, more holistic process – the process of doing, and was beginning to be recognised as an activity in its own right. It was a stage at which we began to see, in a very direct way, the separation of thinking from doing – the separation of hand and brain.

Together with Chris Rawlence and Deborah Hauer, I made a film describing the building of the Cupola and the significance of Brunelleschi's methods for the development of our science and technology, in particular our manufacturing technology. We describe in the film the controversy which surrounded this emergent way of separating "knowing from doing", and we describe a major research project to design and now implement a form of technology which builds on human skill rather than marginalises it. It seems to me always to be important when one identifies a problem of some kind, to immediately begin to look at processes which will transform the problem into some kind of solution. There were, however, other aspects of Brunelleschi's work which time and resources did not allow us to cover in the film. You see Brunelleschi was not only a great designer and architect arising out of the craft tradition (in which he had served his time as a goldsmith). He was also the inventor in 1425 of the technique of linear perspective.

We normally associate perspective with Alberti, because he wrote a treatise on painting, *De Pictura*, which was published in 1435, in which he detailed the notion of perspective.

Over the past five hundred years, our culture has come to

accept perspective as a universally "good thing". We have absorbed its inner meaning into the vernacular. We chide people and tell them they really must "see things in perspective". If somebody is incorrectly judging a situation, we caution them they must "get it into perspective". That is the given and the accepted wisdom. We no longer even think of the implications of the word and its concept. It is so interwoven into our way of thinking and our culture as a whole, that we are really not conscious of what it is doing to us as human beings.

As with the given wisdom in the case of "science", the given wisdom in the case of "education" and the notion of the "school", so also I see "perspective" as very double edged and rife with debilitating and downright dangerous aspects.

Let me return briefly to my fascination with 15th Century Florence to try and explain my concerns and how those concerns affect the way we view the world and our relationship to it.

Prior to the time of Brunelleschi and Alberti, new European drawings embodied a conscious sense of perspective. Drawings of the siege of a city would usually show those inside and outside the fortifications as being of equal size and apparently at an equal distance from the painter. It was as though the painter was looking at each of them individually and was not distancing himself or herself from those being viewed in varying degrees.

The same lack of perspective was evident in the drawing of cities. By our modern sense of what a drawing or painting should be, these early paintings appear simply to be an assembly of buildings as though the painter was representing what it might be like to walk about the city experiencing the structures from many sides rather that from one single distant vantage point.

The frescos in Florence show panaramas of the city represented in this way. Those drawings speak to me of a world in which we felt the presence of ourselves to be in the midst of things. By the 1480s there were drawings of Florence which depicted the city in a very different way indeed. Though the painter was no longer in amongst the structures of the city, but was a remote spectator at some distant point, taking a birds-eye view on the city and seeing it "in perspective", it was as though we had raised ourselves above the city, that we were distant from it but above everything else, we were out of active contact with it. We were a distant spectator of the city.

Psychologically, this began to inculcate to our consciousness, the notion that we can only properly understand things if we distance ourselves from them, if we remove ourselves from the tactile and audio feedbacks of the world around us. It is a world which is "out of touch" in the deepest sense of the word. It is a world understood only through one sense – the eyes. It is a world ideally suited to an explanation rooted in geometry. It no longer involves our ears or our hands. We no longer feel the texture of the city's walls, the roughness of its cobblestone streets, the echoes as we walk through its alleyways. We no longer smell the inviting aroma of its bakeries, its restaurants, or the unpleasantness of its sewers and fumes. We no longer hear the sounds of its children at play; the laughter or the anger of its citizens. It is in fact, no longer a 'living' place. It is the world, distant and abstract, as seen through the eyes of the increasingly remote spectator.

To draw in perspective, we need to use a modern term: a vanishing point. Alberti used to refer to this as a centre point which, in his time was known as *punto di fuga* – the point of flight. I regard this as deeply symptomatic of what has been happening to us. We are taking flight from reality and moving into high level abstractions.

The concept of the spectator and of distance has both a physical and a psychological dimension. If in a crowded city a funeral cortège passes us on the road, we are hardly conscious that the vehicle leading the cortège is a hearse and that within it is a coffin and within that is a corpse. Although we are physically close to the funeral, we are distanced from it psychologically since we do not know the person who has died. If, however, a friend or close relative dies, even in a distant city or on another continent, we feel a sense of bereavement and personal loss. In that case we are physically distant but psychologically close.

There is a spectrum of closeness. If we say to our colleagues at work that we won't be in during the afternoon because we have to go to a funeral and they express sympathy, we may sometimes respond "Oh its only a distant relative", thereby defining distance as a level of involvement. In general, when we are both physically and psychologically close to a situation, there is intensity and deep connectedness.

If distance, perspective and the window lead to disconnection and abstraction to the extent that we are indifferent, even to the plight of our fellow species as was the case in the Gulf and Vietnam, then it is not surprising that we display such alarming indifference to other species, plants and material. Yet the basis of our present scientific methodology is to further distance us from the world around us. It is to be found vividly in the origins of what we now would regard as modern science.

Copernicus and Galileo essentially instructed us that we

could only understand the motion of Earth and its place in the universe if we analysed it from the perspective (!) of somebody standing on the Sun. We were being told then, and modern science continually tells us now, that we cannot understand the Earth by being in it and of it. Only when we distance ourselves from it can we see it in perspective and take a rational and objective view of it.

The same is now being said in respect of the steps we must take to heal the planet we have so seriously wounded. Satellites will circle the earth and with advanced surveillance and monitoring equipment, will gather data on global warming, atmospheric changes, concentrations of pollution, water supply problems, growing "desertification" and the destruction of the rain forests. The data will be beamed back and with very sophisticated imaging systems, we will see on screens (windows!) in a dazzling array of colours the results of our own environmental vandalism displayed graphically.

In the midst of all this technological wonderment, it is easy to forget that it has all become necessary as a result of our rapacious approach to nature and our uncaring attitude to the flora and fauna around us. As one gazes at the images through the window of our television screens, it is difficult indeed to relate what we are seeing to the declining number of butterfly species visiting our garden or to the situation in some parts of the great United States where there are now beginning to be feuds over the supply of something as mundane as clean drinking water.

The images sometimes depict Earth as a globe with changing colours on the surface in a manner not unlike the array of colours on bubbles one blew as a child. It is true that these powerful information processing and display systems do provide us with an 'overview' and lots of data. However, unless those overviews and the dangers they imply can be related to the way people live and use technology, their exercise is unlikely to be effective. The challenge is to transform the masses of scientific data into wisdom and then into sensitive action.

There is a great distance indeed between seeing on the screen an area of green in South America being gradually penetrated by an expanding area of red, and understanding that this represents the depletion of the rainforests. Furthermore, it is not easy to relate the forms of economics, technology, ways of living we have developed, and material expectations we hold so dear, to environmental damage. Perhaps we need to reflect upon the number of discarded and unrecycled issues of *The Guardian* that contain the pulp equivalent of one tree.

Unless mechanisms exist for consciousness raising programmes and cultural changes, the image on the screen will remain nothing much more than another form of intellectual computer game. What will matter is how people "on the ground" react to what is happening to their environment and how they transform into action and changed patterns of consumption their concerns when they see the flora and fauna around them being so wantonly destroyed. Until they know and understand and feel that by damaging nature they are indeed damaging themselves, little will be altered.

If the global view transmitted by the technology helps in that process, then it is worthwhile but only then, and we may perhaps lay the basis for a society in which we can think globally and act locally. The destruction of the rain forests denies the rest of the world some of its cleansing and purifying lungs just as the consequences of Chernobyl have spread internationally. Likewise, the melting of the ice caps will raise the sea levels worldwide. The awesome power of our technology is no longer confined to one region or nation and is no respector of national boundaries or individual cultures. It forces upon us a vivid lesson of our interdependence as a species worldwide and our dependence on nature itself.

These huge problems cannot be solved by some slick technological fix. Indeed, science and technology is far too arid and shallow a soil in which to transplant the roots of our humanity and civilisation. Science can only be but one part of a wider cultural and industrial renaissance which will rekindle in us a love and respect for nature and a desire to deal frugally with the materials around us. This will require both modesty and insight from our species and an understanding of the limitations of scientific and technological solutions. It seems clear to me that we are now far too smart scientifically to be able to survive much longer without wisdom!

It would of course be ludicrous to suggest abandoning that form of science which sprang from the insights of Copernicus and Galileo and I am not suggesting that we do so. What I do suggest, however, is that this is just one method of knowing the world and our place in it. We need now to create a great historical synthesis in which we unite the observer and the participant, the distant and the near, the objective and the subjective, the intellectual and the tactile.

It is now far too late to win back that form of closeness to nature which our early hunter/gatherer predecessors must have known. They depended on nature and they knew that they depended on it as manifest by their rituals and beliefs. They were close to the heartbeat of nature and its seasons and its moods. They were close to and they respected the species they hunted. Some of the North American Indians knew the traits of individual animals they pursued in a relationship that was sustainable in an ecological sense. Their lifestyle was to live with nature, to see themselves as part of nature rather than an outsider concerned with its control and exploitation. Their animistic beliefs provided a safeguard against the ravaging of nature which is now so deeply wounding our planet. We will somehow have to link scientific knowledge with the deep insights of primitive people who love their forests, those lungs of our world, and who know intimately the varieties of plants, insects and even reptiles which are the source of a vast array of herbal and natural cures which we should all be preserving for future generations.

The future is really going to depend on our ability to create a culture in which we can link, in a great consummation of traditions, the mind of the scientist and the heart of the Peruvian Indian.

This is aptly named, because it coincides with the stage at which we began to take flight from the concrete and specific to a point where we could act as a spectator from without. But it was also much more than that. Alberti, in describing how to produce drawings in perspective, pointed out that he draws a rectangle of whatever size drawing he requires "Which I regard as an open window through which the subject to be painted is seen".

The metaphor of the window recurs right up to the present day. We talk about windowing techniques in Computer Graphics and windows of opportunity, but it also has a much deeper significance. It constitutes a separation between the observer and that which is being observed. More particularly, a window means that we perceive the world around us through one sense only – that of vision.

The Window of Disaster

A closed window normally excludes smell, it reduces and in some cases excludes sound and it separates us physically from the real world. When we sit at a window and observe wind and rain, we experience a very different sensation from actually feeling the rain trickle through our hair. It is different also from the feeling of gusts of wind tugging at our coat. The window is in fact a barrier between us and the real world. Double glazed windows are used in cities to give us the impression that there is no noise but the moment we open the window, it comes hurtling in at us. We get a view but only a one dimensional view.

Initially, Alberti's window might have been said to be an open window. Gradually, however, he expressed the idea that the window could be viewed as a filter or as a veil. He said "It is like this: a veil loosely woven of thin thread. Dye it whatever colour you please. Divide it by the thicker threads into as many parallel square sections as you like and stretch it on a frame. I set this up between the eye and the object to be represented, so that the visual pyramid passes through the loose weave of the veil."

This was on the one hand laying out the basis on which a drawing would be constructed in perspective, but on the other hand it was also pointing out that depending on the veil or grid we used on the window, we would perceive the same thing differently. We may construct cultural filters or as I have been suggesting, we have, in Western society, now constructed a form of mathematical or scientific filter which only lets through that which the filtering mechanism allows.

This way of thinking laid the basis for television screens as windows and computer screens as windows. Indeed, many people refer to the television as being their window on the world, but it is a world without smell, without touch and it is also a world which results in a feeling of separation and of distance. The more distant something is, the less connected we feel with it and our perception of it is grossly changed.

We find the emergence of the sense of difference in writers from Shakespeare to the present day. In *King Lear*, Edgar says to Gloucester "the fisherman that walk upon the beach appear like mice" and if something appears merely as a mouse, our perception of its importance and its relationship to ourselves is, of course, dramatically changed.

Shortly after the War, there appeared a book describing bombing raids over Germany. The author, who was, I believe, a pilot, pointed out that in one of his missions he was to bomb a tunnel. As he flew along the railway line towards the tunnel, he passed a train. If he bombed the entrance to the tunnel the train would be unable to enter and presumably would stop. From his height in the sky, the train looked like a worm inching its way towards a hole in the ground. He recounts in the book how he decided to overfly the tunnel, come from the opposite direction, close the exit and then fly over the tunnel. By this time the train would have entered it and then he would close the other end.

It all sounded very much like getting rid of an insect, but what was happening was that hundreds of people were being buried alive in that tunnel. I doubt if that pilot, hardened though he might have been by the brutalities of war, would have been willing to bury alive two or three hundred people one by one, to see them struggling to get to air, gasping as they choked and writhing in agony. But seeing it as an abstraction from a distance, it seems not a particularly unreasonable thing to do. It is only when we bring ourselves closer to the passengers, submerge ourselves in their midst, that we can fully understand the horrific nature of the deed.

Likewise, we are now capable of doing horrific things to nature and its creatures and disastrously waste its materials because we have separated ourselves from it. Our murderous attitude to other human beings was expressed so poignantly by Graham Greene's charismatic villain, Harry Lime in *The Third Man*. The scene is on top of the ferris wheel, way above the ground. His friend has challenged him about the hideousness of his behaviour in peddling drugs which have disfigured and killed hundreds of young children. He has just seen the vividness of that by visiting a children's hospital. Harry Lime asks his friend to come to the window and from the height above the playground points to the distant children playing far below. Then he looks down and says: "What does it matter if one of those specks ceases to move?" The physical distance has become a psychological one and the terrible act of extinguishing a child's lamp of life appears as a mere cleansing operation. In Vietnam, pouring yellow agent and napalm on the Vietcong was to 'clean out the gooks' – rather like spraying insecticide on infested crops!

This form of abstraction reached its pinnacle in the first Gulf War. Day in day out, members of the public sat mesmerised in front of televisions as they witnessed the awesome precision of delivery systems which gave a new and perverse meaning to the term "surgical". It induced a voyeuristic mixture of fascination and horror. Fascinated and morally anaesthetised by the abstraction of the moving particles on our television screens (The Window) in what seemed to be one of the most sophisticated electronic wargames one might purchase from our friendly computer store, and then horrified to suddenly realise that the little distant puff of smoke as the missile homed, signalled another consignment of mangled bodies in what would ultimately reach a body count of some hundred thousands.

Pilots spoke of going on 'turkey shoots' along the road of retreat from Kuwait. In Vietnam, a pilot observed that because of the height, the ground below looked like a carpet and dropping the Napalm was like dropping a match on a distant carpet. In the subsequent photographs of the war, we saw the appalling spectacle of half naked children running with the clinging, burning napalm still flaming on their backs. Very few soldiers, however brutalised, would be capable of taking a child and putting burning napalm on its back and those who would be willing to do it would be treated as war criminals and as perverts, whereas in the abstraction of modern war, it is feasible to do so with little personal consequence.

Our spectator status diminishes us and reduces us to a unidimensional understanding of the world, but it also damages us psychologically. The technologies we are now developing reflect that damage and that distortion. For example, in the military/industrial complex we have developed sophisticated 'seek and destroy' systems. These are linked to surveillance technologies which can intercept faint signals emanating from enemy controlled centres. Once they are located, a payload of destruction is delivered with uncanny accuracy; in some cases literally "arriving through the front door". Yet throughout the world, we are incapable of hearing the dying whimpers of dehydrated children, as the plight of the Kurds has shown.

CHAPTER 14

PATHS NOT TAKEN

Estragon: "That wasn't such a bad little canter."
Vladimir: "Yes, but now we'll have to find something else."
Waiting for Godot, Samuel Beckett

We now draw to the close of the most extraordinary millennium in human history. The path we have taken has been strange and tortuous. It has been productive and destructive, progressive and regressive and always double-edged. It gave us the beauty that is Venice and the hideousness that is Chernobyl. It produced the musical delights of Mozart and the stench of Bergen-Belsen. It afforded us the linguistic labyrinth of Shakespeare but the anihilation of the Aboriginal people with their dream-time culture. Röntgen discovered X-rays with their diagnostic potential, but we also devised the scientific womb which gave birth to the carnage at Hiroshima. We developed the capacity to restore sight to the blind in opthalmic surgical departments but we blinded people at Bhopal. We can justifiably be proud of the techniques of immunisation but should be ashamed that we opened the Pandora's box of biological and chemical weapons. On the curious path to our Damascus, many indeed have been the "paths not taken".

Our faltering steps took us from feudal societies to the growth of the Tuscany city states and the Renaissance. We facilitated the emergence of a science which we were assured would abolish superstition and the mysterious and

165

replace it with the rational and the objective. We witnessed the decline of religion as a leading edge in society and its replacement with the new religion, science.

Above all, we saw the growth of industrial society. It started out unpretentiously as clock mechanisms, architecture, optical instruments and early metallurgy. Gradually, steam power puffed its way into our lives and by the beginning of the industrial revolution it was gathering momentum and "wasn't such a bad little canter".

The industrialisation soon accelerated to a stampede which trampled across the face of the countryside and crushed within its wheels much of our humanity. The last fifty years have seen it unleash its hurricane destructiveness.

To date, a good measure of the development of our industrial society has been the rate at which we consume energy. During the past seventy five years we have consumed (I would prefer to say 'wasted') more than the sum of all the energy consumed throughout the whole course of human history up to about 1920. That is truly something awesome to contemplate. We have depleted our fossil fuel heritage as though we understood the Earth to be some kind of gigantic power station of infinite supply from which we could continue to draw energy to the end of time.

In parallel with this, we have scavenged the Earth's mineral resources in a manner which prompted Loren Eiseley to describe Western industrial man as a "world eater". Generations of artists, poets and writers have tried to alert us to the catastrophe of our own making in voices that ranged from musical analogy to brutal frankness. D H Lawrence put it thus:

"There, in the world of the mechanical greedy, greedy\ mechanism and mechanised greed, sparkling with lights and gushing hot metal and roaring with traffic, there lay the vast evil thing, ready to destroy whatever did not conform. Soon it would destroy the wood, and the bluebells would spring no more. All vulnerable things must perish under the rolling and ramming of iron."

To continue in this manner is simply not an option. Those who say that we can or still behave as if we can, are now a serious threat to our continued existence. We may have got away with it for a few hundred years and in the process have extracted some material advantages, but that phase is rapidly coming to a close one way or the other. We must agree with Vladimir when he says "Yes, but now we'll have to find something else".

There is now a galaxy of reasons why we must urgently do so. If we maim our planet much further we will mortally wound it. If the planet dies, we die. We continue to decimate those cultures and people who love, respect, protect and live in harmony with the flora and fauna around them.

In the Peruvian Amazon, of the forty five thousand people who inhabited their Huitotos territories at the turn of the Century, there are now only five hundred left. One of the leaders, Evaristo Nugkuag Ikanan, recently pointed out that the colonisers "showed more respect to the animal world than to the lives of our ancestors. Then there were the religious missionaries who, in the process of supposedly saving our souls, destroyed our spirit."

The sages in the Himalayas point out that trees are the givers of the ten important gifts: life-giving oxygen, water, soil, food, fruit, medicine, fibre and shade while the tree is living, and timber and firewood when it is dead. The enduring nature of this forest culture for its people was expressed beautifully when one of them said: "The stream of these ideas remains floating in the hearts of the people since time immemorial". As yet, we have not found, if indeed we were even seeking, a way of creatively merging this inherent ecological understanding with our own scientific tradition. Meantime, we are killing the planet slowly but surely. Of course, we may do it very quickly by accident. We still have enough nuclear weapon "capability" for one Hiroshima every day for the next four thousand years!

Part of the problem is that our educational system and our culture convey to us the false notion that everything worth while and beneficial was discovered this century. We are confronted with a form of present-tense technology which obliterates the past and mortgages what remains of the future. It is said that we must continue in this way, for we cannot, as we are so often reminded, turn back or even stop the clock. However, as Jakob von Uexkull has pointed out, very few of us would buy a clock which cannot be reset as and when required. One wonders how long we will be prepared to put up with a system which has become so powerless, confused, sterile and imprisoned by its own institutions as to be unable to offer us more than different varieties of clocks all out of control!

We are locked into a sort of crazy bicycle economy where we have to keep frantically pedalling forward, for if we ever slow down the bicycle will topple over. Islands of sanity do remain, but the seas of destructiveness and irresponsibility are ever rising to submerge them. What, in all the midst of this chaos, can we as individuals hope to do? Buckminster Fuller pointed out that the scales are now so evenly balanced between disaster and survival that every single individual can make a crucial difference. I shall attempt to describe some steps we might take individually and collectively.

Firstly, let us consider what state of mind we are in individually. In spite of all the technological power and all the means of analysis, information retrieval and decision-making systems, we have never felt as part of humanity so insecure, so helpless and so despairing of the future. Mother Theresa of Calcutta pointed out when she visited Europe "Here I find a different kind of poverty, a poverty of loneliness, of being unwanted; a spiritual poverty and that is the worst illness in the world today".

The forms of science and technology which have done so much obvious damage to nature and the environment are also doing us, as individuals, damage on a massive scale. In our technological narcissism we have created technologies in our own image and then so titivated and perfected that technology that we come to see it as superior to ourselves. The Polish author Lesz, expressed it prosaically when he said: "Technology is on its way to reach such a perfection that human beings believe they can do without themselves".

We are well on the way to succeeding in transforming Mary Shelley's story of 1816 into a reality. Frankenstein, if we remember, is made in the image of his creator, Dr Victor Frankenstein. He is the product of his designer's own desire to create a new race of beings. He engages in the animation of inanimate objects. This is the conferring of life on machines as we diminish ourselves.

The other monsters we encounter in ghost stories or fairytales and in legends look like dragons, gush flames or, if in human form, walk through walls and float in the air. We have no idea how they are made or where they come from.

Frankenstein is altogether different. The difference is that he is in an awful, grotesque way like us. In Mary Shelley's story we do know exactly where he comes from. He has been made by us. He is in every sense of the word man-made.

We are now coming very close to creating our present day Frankensteins. There is already talk of 'guilds of robots' which will share a common culture, will interact with each other, will browse rather than retrieve information. Artificial intelligence devices at present under development, it is said, will very soon be in a form to surpass our own intelligence as we become more passive and they become more active. We are assured that if we design them properly and imbue in them the correct objectives and instincts, they will look after us and take care of us. This is seen by some as a form of technological Darwinism in which intelligence, having migrated from primitive animal forms to human beings, now realises that they too have outlived their historical 'leading edge-ism' and so intelligence is migrating to machines.

I find it not surprising that we have reached this extraordinary historical position. I believe we have been asking the wrong questions of science and technology and I find it therefore not surprising that we have come up with the wrong answers. The means we have been using are part of the problem. Science on its own is inadequate and in many cases inappropriate to investigate its own deficiencies. To attempt to do so is like looking for the dark with a powerful light.

We now live in a binary age of great danger and extraordinary opportunity. For the past fifty years we have walked a precarious tight rope between the two. Throughout that period, the balance has been shifting towards the former and away from the latter. It is as though we have been unconsciously laying out an elaborate minefield armed with the most lethal high explosives and biological devices right across the only exit from the past and into the future. Consciously or unconsciously, we have been engaged in a battle with nature (indeed we always seek to control and exploit it) and our minefield has been securing a region from which we have driven it. At a mundane level, houses, cars, aircraft, almost everything that is man made is constructed to keep out nature, to control it, to oppose and resist it rather than to live with it.

We have been constructing this metaphorical minefield for at least 1000 years but the plans were already fermenting in our Western minds much earlier.

Over that thousand years, each generation has added its own ever more ingenious and ever more destructive devices into this minefield complex. We have now been doing it for so long that we have forgotten the codes we initially used to prime the explosive devices. In our confusion, we have also lost the layout drawings, the mapping, the location and significance of each device. We are therefore now quite incapable of defusing it. It will be necessary to go back to the origins of these ideas, back to the original codes to find out what we have done and learn from the past how we might now undo them.

Few can still accept that this is what must be done. For the majority, so confounded by our technocratic conditioning, the only progress they can see is to further expand the potentially lethal minefield we have been so long constructing. Across the minefield, we can see the as yet unspoiled planes beckoning us to a better future. It is a *carte blanche* terrain on which we can write anew a caring and sustainable cultural and industrial renaissance. We just don't know how to get from where we are to where we need to be.

In all past generations, it tended to be the young who look

forward, in whatever confused sort of way, to the future and its building. For the first time in human history, as far as I can see, the young, in large numbers, now display pessimism, apprehension and downright fear of the future. Statistical evidence from survey after survey supports one's own subjective judgement and anecdotal evidence on this issue.

One of the most sobering experiences for me recently, was a discussion with a sensitive, talented young biophysics student. He put it to me coherently but very sadly, that our species was now doing such damage to the life around it that it would be in the long term interests of the planet if we ceased to exist. Then, he contended, at least the other forms of life would have the opportunity to continue to evolve and this may lead, in some long distant future, to a more caring lead species than the present barbaric one.

Mother nature, that great experimentalist, has now discovered that the material she had chosen to mould into a species "like unto God", is just a murderous preditor. So, she has been quietly weaning us on the hemlock of our own arrogance to facilitate our departure from a scene we have so terribly sullied. There are those who believe that the body of nature now experiences industrialised humanity as a destructive virus which has been attacking it. The reaction of that body has been to rally its natural defences to extinguish the virus. The body is cleansing itself by facilitating the virus in engineering its own demise. They feel we have already reached the point of no return. With famines, wars, drought, AIDS, nuclear weapons, population explosions, pollution and desertification, I can understand such terminal pessimism but I do not share it.

I too am deeply apprehensive, but I do believe that our

species is flexible, adaptive and intelligent enough to realise when it is engineering its own destruction and to take remedial steps. Meantime, the technology with which we have done this to nature has been wreaking a terrible toll on all of us individually and collectively. The modern cities we are constructing do not contain homes but houses and buildings. We experience not communication but noise. Large numbers drift aimlessly and without purpose. With our rationality we have abolished the mystique of a god but have provided nothing in its place but material greed. We suffer the fallout from a data explosion but have little knowledge and are starved of wisdom. We have deep knowledge of slender subjects but lack slender knowledge of deep subjects.

For a thousand years our concern has moved from: "the slenderest knowledge that may be obtained of the deepest things" (Aquinas) to detailed, scientific, mathematically precise knowledge of lesser things. We have moved from knowledge for understanding and conceptualisation to knowledge for manipulation and control. We set out to manipulate and control nature and matter and we ended up controlling society and humans. We have relationships but lack compassion, we have atomised the community and the family and replaced it with the social services departments. Where we used to belong we now have a claimant relationship. Like the old lady who swallowed the spider to catch the fly, we create more technology to simplify the complexity we have already made and thus create a higher level of complexity requiring us to frantically invent yet more technology.

So as we caterpillar our way to the nearest supermarket or to a disconnected, irrelevant task we call a job, we might reflect with T S Eliot:

"Endless invention, endless experiment,
Brings knowledge of motion, but not of stillness;
Knowledge of speech, but not of silence;
Knowledge of words, and ignorance of the Word.
All our knowledge brings us nearer to our ignorance,
All our ignorance brings us nearer to death,
But nearness to death no nearer to God.
Where is the Life we have lost in living?
Where is the wisdom we have lost in knowledge?
Where is the knowledge we have lost in information?
The cycles of heaven in twenty centuries
Bring us farther from God and nearer to the Dust."

A long-standing friend and mentor of mine, Richard Fletcher, said something to the effect that a problem well defined is already halfway towards a solution.

I have attempted up to this point to at least describe, if not define, the problem both implicitly and explicitly, by way of analogy and example. I suspect it is because of my engineering background that I always feel a responsibility to attempt to transform the criticisms I make or the problems I identify into some sort of solution. This means that one attempts to propose practical solutions on however modest and small a scale. If they are ideas that have come of their time, it may be that they will be sparks that start prairie fires. At least one has the opportunity to test them out in practice.

This is important at many levels, not least because it shows a positive and constructive approach to dealing with the problems which surround us. It is therefore different in kind from the hand wringing and wrinkled brow expressions of concern of so many well meaning liberal people. Such expressions of concern are, of course, very much better than no expressions at all, but they do convey a sense that such people are better at saying what they don't want rather than what they do want. This is particularly so when it come to products and technology.

Such an attitude then allows those who wish the juggernaut of technology to continue on its supercharged way, to portray them as negative and a sort of concerned spoilsport. On the other hand, small scale practical projects which arise out of these very same concerns are much more subversive of the given orthodoxy in the sense that they are suggesting what can be done rather than what should not be done. This usually provides for a positive rather than a negative feedback. It helps to give practical expression and even legitimacy to conscious and subconscious concerns which people have long felt about the present course of events.

These practical project examples frequently resonate with doubts and fears people have felt privately, but are loth to express in case they appear to be not quite with it! After all, as is often said "progress is progress", and in its own terms it is always good and positive so, therefore, who dares stand in the way of progress? Practical projects and imaginative proposals for alternatives can help re-define what it is we mean by progress.

I shall describe a few such projects already under way and attempt to describe some future possible ones. No attempt is made here to provide a blueprint for the future. Blueprints can be very dangerous documents indeed. They are usually handed down from on high (from a distance!) by an individual or group which believes it knows how the rest of us should live our lives.

These are the big blueprints, the bureaucratic blueprints. In their nastier forms they provide for the chilling awfulness of the Gulag Archipelago, the human abattoir of the concentration camp, and the precision of the Gulf War. In their benign form, they give us high rise flats, factory schools and the children's homes of social service departments.

The blueprints which really matter are those which are so small as to be invisible in the minds and hearts of masses of people. They provide the common culture, understanding and shared outlook which fuses together in social and creative activities that historically gave us the city states of Tuscany and the uprisings in Eastern Europe.

These are blueprints rooted in the consciousness of people; in their actions, in their dreams and in their culture. They are not instructions from without. They come from within and are then shared and strengthened at the level of the community and the culture. It is to this source of understanding and commitment that we must look for the changes which are now so burningly necessary.

The cynic will ask if ordinary people are capable of taking these initiatives. I must protest that there is no such thing as an ordinary person! At least I have never succeeded in meeting one. All the people I meet are extraordinary, with all kinds of fears, wishes, hobbies, interests, dreams, and aspirations. They are all marvellosly different and each unique. Like the leaves on a tree they are identifiable as a group which defines the species but although they are similar, they are never identical. Secondly, the response of 'ordinary people' will depend in part how issues are presented. An African leader once said:

> "Let your words be so clear and direct and simple that the ideas they represent flow through ordinary people's consciousness as easily and naturally as the wind and the rain flow through the trees."

176

I took him to be advocating the drawing of analogies which resonate in people's consciousness.

So no attempt is made here to present a blueprint but rather to provide some analogies and indicate the kind of cultural outlook and historical tendencies which will provide the fertile soil from which these new ideas will grow. It is notoriously difficult to predict which ideas will flourish. "If you can look into the seeds of time and say which will grow and which will not ...", as Shakespeare reminded us. What I suggest only is that we must urgently rethink our relationship with nature, with each other, with our work and the types of science and technology which increasingly mediate these. I am optimistic that we can do so.

It may be held that this is idealistic. The world today urgently needs idealism and it is a measure of the extent to which we have degenerated that to refer to somebody as an idealist is to insult them. It may appear to be romantic but there is nothing wrong in that so long as we are not foolishly romantic. Each and every one of us is romantic to some degree or other. Being romantic keeps us going, as my colleague Leopold Kohr so mischievously observed:

> "Only to a romantic does life make sense. Starting from nothing and ending in nothing and costing a lot in between is irrational and economically indefensible. Only a romantic sees glory and meaning in the rainbow spanning the two zero magnitudes which mark the beginning and the end."

To start with, I believe we require a different state of mind. We must sever the link between gigantic intervention and progress. We cannot continue the way we are now going. Every labourer digging a tunnel knows that if the roof keeps falling in you stop digging. You've got to think of something else. To say we should stop our frantic linear drive forward is made to sound regressive and backward looking. We are assured that in this age of progress it makes no sense to step back, but as an anthropologist once put it "When you have reached the edge of the abyss, the only thing that makes sense is to step back". Far from an abject, senseless retreat, that is simply a sound tactic.

To do this, we need to re-examine our relationship with nature or, better expressed, we need to understand that we are part of nature. We could do worse than re-examine the notions that so-called primitive people had of the relationship between human beings and the earth. In 1854, Chief Seattle of the Suquamish tribe so beautifully expressed it when the ancestral Indian lands were being taken from the indigenous people and transferred to the federal government in the United States:

> "This we know: the earth does not belong to man, man belongs to the earth. This we know: all things are connected, like the blood which unites one family. All things are connected. Whatever befalls the earth, befalls the sons of the earth. Man did not weave the web of life, he is merely part of it. Whatever he does to the web he does to himself.'

In one of the most terrible crimes in all of human history, we Europeans all but destroyed the diverse Indian tribes in what is now the United States. One of the reasons was to give the land to those who would "utilise it". It was said that the Indians were savages, incapable of adapting to 'progress', but the American Indian's lifestyle was sustainable and their respect for the land and the species they hunted was legendary. Our lifestyle is not sustainable, yet we tend to think of earlier species and of other peoples as becoming extinct because they did not change and adapt. It would be indeed an ironic twist of history if we were to render ourselves extinct by over adaptation to the crudeness of industrialisation!

By intervening on such a massive scale, we create a precariousness which, when something goes even slightly wrong, can be catastrophic for the environment. We may think of the oil spillage from the *Valdez*. Day by day, the ruptures in the pipelines across Siberia are causing equal, or perhaps greater, devastation as oil pollution obliterates flora and fauna and destroys the lifestyle of indigenous people.

It seems as though we are only prepared to take care of species or an environment when it is on the brink of extinction. The response of the military/industrial complex, the vast oil corporations, and the socialist bureacracies in the case of the Soviet Union is to say that they will add yet more safeguards rather than accepting the need to organise our affairs and our industry in a radically different fashion. It seems that it is only when we reach a point of no return, when we have mortally wounded the planet, that we will realise what we have done and start bemoaning our lack of foresight. Yet for those who will but look at the signs, nature is telling us it will be then too late. It is for me as though Lord Tennyson were giving her voice:

"Come not, when I am dead,
To drop thy foolish tears upon my grave,
To trample round my fallen head,
And vex the unhappy dust though wouldst not save.
There let the wind sweep and the plover cry;
But thou, go by."

To change we will require a new morality and a new form of

economics. We do see these already emerging in embryo. There is the Alternative Economic Summit. One of my colleagues, the Chilean economist Manfred Max Neef, is laying the basis for an international doctoral programme in ecological economics. John Davis, a former manager at Shell, has written a book on sustainable management. The list thankfully grows daily.

But it is really to the future generations to which we must look, in particular to young children. Parents should encourage them to respect and enjoy nature. They could help them to make small objects of natural materials, seek in the woods and on the beaches pieces of material which are close to size and which, with the minimum of intervention, can be made into delightful objects. They should encourage them to be involved in the restoration of furniture and equipment so as to extend its life cycle.

The Sunday morning car-boot sale is a novel alternative to the ritual Sunday afternoon drive to the local council's rubbish tip. In some parts of the South of England, they are verging on the respectable. Whereas only three years ago, these 'respectable people', surprised to encounter their even more respectable neighbours, would explain with some embarrassment that they were just getting a few items for the playgroup or, to tinge the excuse with an academic air, 'There might be some interesting books'. Now the boot sale has been elevated to a sort of shared sense of discovery. "Did you see the grand oval table over there? I'm sure the scratches on the surface could be polished out" or "That picture would be worth buying to get the lovely old frame". They are becoming a form of family outing. Even passing remarks such as "That's a lovely piece of oak" or "See this exquisite mother of pearl inlay!" can all subtly convey the message that we don't throw good material on the dump and that these artefacts are worth restoring.

In some of the German cities, the locals, with the agreement of their city council, leave items they wish to dispose of on the pavement outside their houses during the summer on the day before the official collection by the local authority. The predominantly middle class 'shoppers' arrive on foot with their children or by bicycle with the youngest in the carrier seat. Having located something to their taste, if they cannot carry it by hand or on the bike, they will afix a 'reserved for ...' note to the item, go back for their Citroen 2CV to collect it and return home on a slow spring-compressing journey. Little trailers on the bicycles are also favoured for smaller loads. Those items which don't find a taker are left for the council to take to a sorting depot where a selection takes place of those things most easily re-cyclable.

For many of my academic friends in Germany, conspicuous consumption, far from being a pointer to wellbeing and affluence, is regarded as a sign of downright bad taste.

When parents are cooking, repairing, decorating, sowing seeds and transplanting, changing the plugs in the car, they should encourage their children to be involved. Those who are self employed or who have their own small businesses could and should involve their children. As in Zola's *Utopia*, this would begin to lay the basis for manual work and manipulation of materials to rank alongside book learning. 'Intellectual' and technical education could be carried on simultaneously.

Some of the finest craftspeople in Italy still learn their skill in this way. One of their most famous metal engravers expressed surprise at my own surprise to see his six year old daughter producing such beautiful craft objects. "Well of course she can" he explained "As a child in her cot she used to sleep to the tap of my engraving. She absorbed the rhythm of this work from the earliest age". We can so easily underestimate what children absorb simply by "being there" and being involved.

There are exciting projects that schools could undertake. The biologist Dr Anne Powell, with her marvellous pond action programme, has provided us with a project which is at once fun, educational and ecologically beneficial. It is one which could involve children in the form of action and play which in my own childhood I found so useful and informative. Schools could adopt a pond, a section of a stream or a piece of wasteland and organise biology, physics, chemistry and other classes around such a project. It is often stimulating for children to write delightful little poems about nature and the environment and their relationship to it. My experience suggests that large numbers of children do enjoy the metre and rhythm of poetry. This could help resolve the apparent dichotomy that when science advances poetry retreats.

The new requirement for classes in Design Technology could also be used imaginatively. Projects on enviromentally desirable, long life and repairable small products could begin to find expression there. This kind of project learning could and should gradually replace the obsessional, fragmented, exam driven form which is now doing so much damage to our young people.

For those who go into higher education, subjects such as eco-design, sustainable systems and a multi-disciplinary approach should be encouraged. In both schools and universities, a new ethos could be transmitted. In engineering and science departments at the moment the impression is given – convertly and often overtly – that you are not really a suitable person for the coming 21st Century unless you are involved in the exploration of space, the control of nature, the manipulation of data and the exploitation of natural resources.

Against these self defining Olympian tasks, caring for our wounded planet, our diminishing stock of flora and fauna and, of course, looking after each other, is made to look rather pedestrian or downright boring. However, the future of our planet and our species depends on precisely these, yet such concerns are not those on which careers and advancement in the military/industrial complex are built. Indeed, to think about these alternatives, to discuss them with colleagues and seek to create a debate around them, is at best seen as diversionary and, at the worst, is treated as subversive and contrary to the 'company' or the 'national' interest.

In sections of the nuclear industry and parts of the military/industrial complex a form of industrial Eichmannism is required, and any questioning leads to instant dismissal in a process which turns truth on its head, in which the destroyer is portrayed as redeemer and the healer is portrayed as a wrecker.

We need new mechanisms for learning and the transmission of knowledge. For some, universities in revised forms may prove to be suitable. For others, learning-by-doing situations in the form of apprenticeships, learning through community activities, environmental pressure groups or voluntary bodies can be fulfilling and challenging. In all cases, attempting to approach learning and projects in a multidisciplinary way can be highly productive. An attempt might be made once again to allow us to transcend the destructive narrowness of what students in Berlin in the 60's used to call *Fachidioten* (specialist idiots).

We shall have to rekindle in ourselves and our community a respect for diversity both within ourselves and in particular in nature. This will mean confronting the conformity which flows from the notion of the "one best way". Diversity in our flora, fauna, terrain, language and culture is part of our heritage and we should regard it as precious.

The long term future will depend on this diversity both in its genetic and cultural forms. The rate at which we are losing it is mind blowingly fast. For example, in the United States during the last century over seven thousand named varieties of apple were cultivated. Now over six thousand of these are extinct. In Europe, we are converging on the not-so-golden and certainly not delicious 'one best type'. The same is happening with languages. Each language is a different aperture through which to view and understand the world. In Europe, over thirty lesser used languages are now threatened.

Worldwide, languages of ancient origin find that their characters and script are being questioned as inappropriate for computing systems. Technology will again rule the roost. Similar pressure and conformity existed forty or fifty years ago in respect of printing presses. So we have seen the loss of the old Gaelic zoomorphic letters and the German script. Now, even the language rooted in one of the most powerful economies in the world, Japanese, is beginning to come under pressure.

Some predictions suggest that the Japanese characters will be replaced by Roman ones in new technology systems within the next twenty years. Modern Japanese is written with a combination of Kanji Hiragana and Katakana. Kanji (Chinese characters) were developed in China in the 14th Century BC. They then spread to the neighbouring Korean peninsula. Around the beginning of the 3rd Century, Wan

Wani came to Japan from the ancient nation of Kudara in the eastern part of the peninsula. He brought volumes of the *Annalects of Confucius*, a text book for studying Kanji. That was how Kanji was introduced to Japan. It was not, however, extensively used until the 4th and 5th Centuries when there were greater exchanges between Japan and the Korean peninsula.

This gives some slight idea of the origins in antiquity of one part of modern Japanese. Kanjis, unlike our Roman ABC which consists of phonograms (characters or symbols used to represent a word symbol or phononym), are idiograms (a picture or symbol used to represent a thing or an idea but not a particular word or a phrase of it).

So we have a sense of the very different origins, form and representation of this language to that of our own European languages. The character for rest is actually based on the combination of a human sitting beneath a tree. The character conveys a rich image of what rest has meant to us historically. I do believe it will constitute a terrible loss to humanity if such characters were to go and, if they are threatened in such a powerful economy as the Japanese one, what chance have the lingering remnants of the beautiful languages of the North American Indians under the ravages of modernisation?

None of this should be taken to mean that one is opposed in any way to truly international forms of communication, but rather to suggest that this should not be at the expense of other languages and cultures which will provide the rich reservoir of diversity and variety of outlook which will be necessary in future. Unity should never be taken to mean uniformity.

This diversity will be vital as societies are required, through ecological and other pressures, to move from economy of scale to economy of scope; to retain local skills and uses of materials which will provide the craft diversity which will give us the type of products that are beautiful, aesthetically pleasing and will enrich our lives and will be artefacts which we can pass on to our descendents and to future generations.

Every nation in every part of the world has artefacts of that kind. We may think of Japan as Toyota cars, Sony electronics or NEC printers, but they might have come from any place – indeed, their origins were mainly in Europe and America. I would like to see what a Japanese car looks like as distinct from as European-type car made in Japan. Likewise, I would like to see what an Italian city car would look like if it had been designed within the Italian tradition and to suit, for example, Florence (if cars are to be acceptable at all).

That which I would treasure from Japan is Wajimanuri or Wajima Lacquer Ware. Since ancient times, these beautiful artefacts have been produced on the Noto Peninsula, one of Japan's most remote and isolated areas. Terrain and climate made possible the growth of lacquer trees in that area as early as the 8th Century/ Wajima exchanged lacquer with the imperial court in payment for taxes.

In the 17th Century, locals discovered a type of diatomaceous earth in the hills near Wajima. They found it could be hardened by burning and, when mixed with the lacquer, it yielded a degree of hardness which was beyond compare. To this day, producing a single piece of Wajimanuri involves between seventy-five and a hundred and twenty steps, each demanding incredible skill and considerable time. They are objects of astonishing beauty and delicacy and are sought after and treasured by collectors worldwide. It is a sustainable form of production and what a marvellous world it would be if we all respected and treasured the traditional artefatcs that were produced by the different members of the great human family with all its diversity. This could be done in conjunction with modern technology and new products in a process which linked creatively the old and the new, hand and brain.

CHAPTER 15

THE STUFF OF LIFE

"Theory my friend is grey, green is the stuff of life."
Goethe

I would now like to move to consider a few practical examples which might help to illustrate the green 'stuff of life' that encapsulates some of the ideas I have been talking about.

In the mid 70's, I worked at Lucas Aerospace as a senior design engineer. The company decided to embark on a rationalisation programme. It would have meant some four thousand jobs going. A major part of the company's work was in the defence industry. It is, of course, a sad reflection that in our industrial societies some 50% of all our scientists and engineers are involved directly or indirectly in the so-called defence industry. This constitutes a terrible distortion of our productive efforts and resource allocations.

Rather than seek to defend their 'right to work' by demanding more military projects, the workforce at Lucas Aerospace came up with the creative idea of seeking to use their skills and abilities for socially useful production. It is not my intention to recount here the outpouring of creativity and the sense of excitement and involvement which produced a Corporate Plan containing proposals for some 150 socially useful products which could be made in Lucas and elsewhere. The process by which this happened and the nature of the products themselves, I have described in detail in my book *Architect or Bee?*.

The Plan sparked a long overdue discussion about priorities within science and technology and the responsibility of scientists and engineers themselves. It brought out into the open the industrial Eichmannism behind which many scientists and engineers have veiled their moral responsibilities. It highlighted the gaps between that which technology could provide for society and that which it actually was providing for society. The products ranged from small simple devices which would transform the lives of the disabled, through to large scale, environmentally desirable forms of transport and manufacturing technologies which would enhance human skill rather than destroy it.

Many of the products proposed are now being manufactured worldwide. The process used in drawing up the Plan was one of its most interesting aspects. Firstly, it was conveyed by the Combine Committee to all the different factories that everybody, whether a manual worker or a senior design engineer, had something useful to contribute to the proposal. Secondly, people were encouraged to think of themselves in their dual role, both as producers and as consumers. Thirdly, there was no attempt to compress the expression of creativity into the conventional academic modes.

Thus a deliberate attempt was made to ensure that we did not confuse linguistic ability with intelligence, as the chattering classes so often do. Most people express their intelligence through what they do and how they do it rather than the way they write and talk about it. Some people, for example, produced small models of the products they wished to propose. Others made sketches. Still further groups simply came and spoke about their ideas. There were those who produced conventional drawings and presented them in the conventional form.

The process showed in embryo what would be possible if resources and support were available to involve people in thinking about their communities and the products they required in a process in which they could play a role in the form they felt most appropriate to themselves, creating their own agendas as they went along. For example in Lucas, employees sought the views of the communities in which they were located. This met with varying degrees of success. Some communities did not have a tradition of going to meetings.

Meetings of this kind are often organised in a very hierarchical way with key speakers telling everybody else what they should be doing and deigning to answer a few questions at the end. They do not provide situations in which people can share ideas more freely. They are also often incredibly boring. The situation was different when there were small pieces of equipment and prototypes present which the public could discuss and suggest amendments or alternatives. In one town, Hemel Hempstead, where it proved to be almost impossible to get a meeting, a road/rail vehicle which had been built by the workforce in conjunction with Richard Fletcher from the North East London Polytechnic, was driven down to the marketplace and, with audio and other visual aids, members of the public could come in and discuss what alternative products they felt should be produced. In one day alone, over four hundred visitors proposed various alternative products.

There was then the excitement of the workforce making things which they believed in and doing it in their own way and on their own terms. This was very much the case when components were being made for some of the prototypes. Normally, when industrial workers make components, they have little idea where they are going to be used and certainly have no opportunity of testing out the prototypes. This work is carried out by specialist departments. In this case, workers were working evening and weekends to produce prototypes and a commitment and excitement prevailed which I can not adequately convey but which will be sensed by those who have read *Zen and the Art of Motorcyle Maintenance*.

The catalytic effect of the Plan was extraordinary, with projects which emulate its ideas taking place in many countries throughout the world. What became absolutely clear as the work progressed is that we do now have it within our grasp to feed the hungry, to make the lame walk and the blind see. That is no longer a technical question, it is one of political will, morality and compassion.

The concept of socially useful production provides also a useful framework in which to think of providing fulfilling, challenging work for large numbers of the unemployed, rather than subjecting them to the degradation and suffering of unemployment.

Related activities continue to develop. There is the London Innovation Charitable Trust which has assisted in the development of products ranging from variable geometry seating systems for severely disabled children where, in order to support the body, the seating system must be close fitting and supportive. However, as the child grows, different proportions are required so, as with clothing, a non adjustable chair would have to be replaced at quite short intervals. With the variable geometry seating, a chair can 'grow' through its adjustable elements as the child develops. The end product is beautifully designed with bright colours so there is nothing of the stench of Victorian charity about it. It comes supplied in a flat pack so that parents and child together can build "your chair".

Such seating systems could also be of more universal significance given the huge demographic changes taking place in the industrialised countries. Given the growing numbers of old people, such seating systems would also provide support for them as part of wider schemes and uses of technology which would help older people to be active, committed and independent rather than being institutionalised in their twilight years. So they could be active and involved much more fully, realising "How dull it is to pause, to make an end, to rust unburnished not to shine in use".

Roger Coleman, one of those involved and author of the book *An Epitaph to Skill* is now leading a major project at the Royal College of Art on 'Products and Design for an Ageing Population'. The Innovation Trust is also helping with the development of the Lynch Motor, a permanent magnet motor which significantly reduces energy consumption. In order to draw it fully to the attention of the public, it was used to power a boat with which Lady Arran recently broke the World Speed Record for electrically powered vehicles on water. This further illustrates the extent to which all kinds of people can and should be involved in the development of such products. Lady Arran was 72, so there was no concession either to age or sex!

Brian Padgett, who also worked at Lucas, has helped to set up the Technology Exchange. This is a non-profit organisation which has had funding from the EEC SPRINT Programme. They produce a quarterly catalogue with some 250 product proposals which could be manufactured under licence or on some other collaborative basis. Last year, the TECHNOSHOP had on offer, some 5000 products from around the world.

All of these developments have a growing significance at a time when there is a real possibility for defence cuts. Too often, activities have concentrated on the politics of conversion, the economics of conversion and even the psychology of conversion but precious little on conversion itself. The strength of the Lucas Plan was that it produced prototypes to demonstrate in practice what the alternatives could look like. Properly used, those skills which made possible the Oscar performance of destruction during the Gulf War, could be redeployed to provide products which will enhance life and reduce the damage to the planet. So one is talking about very different products with different value systems built in at the design stage.

Arising from the work on the prototypes in the Lucas Plan, it was possible to draw up a list of some of the attributes which make a product socially useful. These are presented below:

1. The process by which the product is identified and designed is itself an important part of the total process.

2. The means by which it is produced, used and repaired should be non-alientating.

3. The nature of the product should be such as to render it as visible and understandable as is possible and compatible with its performance requirements.

4. The product should be designed in such a way as to make it repairable.

5. The process of manufacture, use and repair should be such as to conserve energy and materials.

6. The manufacturing process, the manner in which the product is used and the form of its repair and final disposal should be ecologically desirable and sustainable.

7. Products should be considered for their long-term characteristics rather than short-term ones.

8. The nature of the products and their means of production should be such as to help and liberate human beings rather than constrain, control and physically or mentally damage them.

9. The production should assist co-operation between people as producers and consumers, and between nation states, rather than induce primitive competition.

10. Simple, safe, robust design should be regarded as a virtue rather than complex 'brittle' systems.

11. The product and the processes should be such that they can be controlled by human beings rather than the reverse.

12. The product and processes should be regarded as important more in respect of their use value than their exchange value.

13. The products should be such as to assist minorities, disadvantaged groups and those materially and otherwise deprived.

14. Products for the Third World which provide for mutually non-exploitative relationships with the developed countries are to be advocated.

15. Products and processes should be regarded as part of culture, and as such meet the cultural, historical and other requirements of those who will build and use them.

16. In the manufacture of products, and in their use and repair, one should be concerned not merely with production, but with the reproduction of knowledge and competence.

Such products will be vitally important if we are firstly to limit and then reverse the damage we are doing to the environment. It is true of course, that population control programmes are absolutely essential. However, even if the world's population were today reduced by 50% this would still not be sustainable if each of them assumed that they could consume energy and material as they do in the United States. It is not the huge polulations in China that are causing the massive damage to the environment at this stage but the minorities in the developed countries, particularly in the United States.

The concept of socially useful production applies not only to products in the conventional manufacturing sense but also to the built environment.

CHAPTER 16

A HUMAN SCALE

Ten or fifteen years ago, there was a big campaign in what was then West Berlin against a huge roadway system which was going through a residential area. One of the posters at the time showed a small child playing with a ball on a little patch of green with some houses in the background. Between that child and another one was this huge motorway complex with cars flying in every direction. The second child, obviously keen to join the first at play, has no idea how to cross this jungle of roads and so with capped hand shouts "How did you get over there?" The first child responds: "I was born here!"

The response reminded us that cities are supposed to be for people but are now of such a form that it seems unnatural to be born and live in them. They are monuments to the technological societies that have produced them. They are constructed as machines. Fritz Lang's *Metropolis* conveyed this vividly but could not have anticipated the levels of hideousness to which we would descend. When the Prince of Wales spoke about the wanton destruction that has taken place in the United Kingdom in the name of progress, and the sheer unadulterated ugliness and mediocrity of modem buildings and housing estates, the response indicated the widespread public concern about the monstrosities being produced in the name of architecture. He pointed out:

"As a result of thirty years of experimenting with revolutionary building materials and novel ideas, burning all the rulebooks and purveying the theory that man is a machine, we have ended up with Frankenstein monsters devoid of character, alien and largely unloved except by the professors who have been concocting these horrors in their laboratories and even find their own creations a bit hard to take after a while".

In our blind rush forward to technological giganticism, we have lost our concept of buildings on a human scale which arise out of the master builder craft tradition with its well developed sense of shape, size and form; the types of buildings which the geographer Pausanias would say later of Greek architecture: "When they were new they looked already ancient. Now that they are old they still look new."

To question what is happening to our city centres is to expose oneself to the psychological intimidation of being unable to understand the nature of progress. For too long we have allowed the technocrats and the vast corporations to define what it is that constitutes progress. New buildings could and should be built in such a form as to provide for longevity, which honours and respects those who look at them and enter them and in their construction and use are energy efficient. Furthermore, progress does not mean tearing down existing, beautifully proportioned buildings so that we can live in the 1990s.

We could learn much in this regard from the Tuscan cities. Siena retains its sense of proportion, its Piazzas, the form of its buildings with many of them tastefully refurbished inside to avail of those aspects of our modern technology whilst honouring the heritage of architecture which earlier generations have given us. This is in glaring contrast to what are now referred to as the recyclable buildings, which fit in

197

with short term, build-and-demolish cycles.

One of my academic commitments is with the University of Urbino. It is essentially a city of the 15th Century, a creation of the renaissance. It is the city of Raphael and Federico Barocci. It provides a powerful sense of continuity with its own artistic and cultural past. Its buildings, from the magnificent Ducal Palace to its small individual dwellings resonate the sense of proportion, skill and loving care of the craftsmen who constructed it. It contains one of Italy's oldest universities, has numerous academies of art, study centres and institutions which attract student scholars, artists and tourists from all over the world. It is a living, dynamic city, not a museum city.

The university department where I am involved is housed in a beautiful ancient building. The scale and proportion and external structure is as it was hundreds of years ago. It has been lovingly restored inside with a layout and use of materials which pays homage to the craftsmen who built the original yet makes sensitive use of modern equipment and facilities. It is a superb synthesis of the best of the past and the present.

In the case of Siena and cities such as Urbino, it is not the case that these are some kind of glorified art galleries and museum cities jealously protected by a small artistic and intellectual elite. The citizens of these cities love and enjoy them and have understood that progress does not have to mean vandalising our heritage from the past.

But these cities and these structures already exist. What options are open for those whose countries are developing and who require that most basic of human needs, housing, for their people. As I have suggested throughout, technology, artefacts and infrastructure should reflect local traditions and culture and make use of locally available materials. My fellow Alternative Nobel Prize recipient, the late Dr Hassan Fathi, embodied in the field of architecture that blend of respect for materials, the environment, artistry and people which I have been attempting to allude to throughout this book. He taught at the faculty of Fine Arts in Cairo, serving as the head of its architecture department. He drew upon the knowledge embodied in the traditional architectural heritage and in the craft skills of Egypt to design and build housing for people which combined economic, social and aesthetic considerations. He transformed his ideas into practice with the building of the village of New Gournia in the Nile Valley. His deep concern has been to provide housing for the 900 million people in the Third World who are doomed to premature death because of bad housing alone, quite apart from deaths from malnutrition, dehydration and disease.

We are not here talking about shoddy, makeshift, shanty town-type accommodation but buildings built cheaply and with craft skills which respect those who will live in them as is the case with some of the dwellings still to be found in the Tuscan city states. His approach is direct and clear:

> "We must subject technology and science to the economy of the poor and the penniless. We must add the aesthetic factor, because the cheaper we build, the more beauty we should add to respect man. When man built on his own he used to beautify everything with his own hands."

He condemns the notion of the 'one best way' and the idea that you design one house and multiply it in its millions whether it be Europe, Africa or India since, as he puts it, "Using concrete does not allow any manipulation of space or articulation of the material". He says: "I would like to introduce in our villages and our cities, musicality and harmonics".

The basic material he uses is clay or mud brick.

> "The material is amorphous, neutral. With half a cubic metre of clay, Rodin made 'The Thinker'. The palaces of the Pharoahs were all in mud brick. In New Mexico, we have a style of architecture all in mud brick from the time of the Indians".

He points out that great structures built of this material have lasted from antiquity. In Egypt, some of the techniques go back to the third dynasty, something like five thousand years ago. He points out that in the fourth century AD, the Christians, when they were persecuted by the Romans, fled into the desert. Though they had nothing but the material around them, they built some two hundred and fifty complex structures, all with vaulted domes, using mud brick from under their feet. These structures are still standing!

Hassan Fathi has had the wisdom of seeing the possibility of combining the modern science of soil mechanics and structures, with the skill of master masons. The buildings he produces are individualised to suit the family and their requirements.

> "A village society takes long to measure and needs more subtle instruments than a tape measure. One thing was clear from the start, that each family must be designed for separately."

He pointed out that their experience in Egypt showed the importance of using local materials and building techniques which accorded with geographical and environmental conditions. He compared ultra-modern pre-fabricated buildings with those constructed of mud brick. The air temperatures in the pre-fabricated house were seven degrees centigrade higher in April than in the mud brick one. The temperature in the mud brick house didn't fluctuate more than two degrees in twenty-four hours and never came outside the acceptable temperature zone. In the ultra-modern concrete model, the temperature didn't enter into the appropriate zone except during one hour in the morning and one hour in the evening. It was, at some times of the day, even higher than the outside temperature! Such houses would require elaborate heating, ventilating and cooling.

He sees the teams required to design and build such structures as a harmonious whole.

> "The cellist would be the soil engineer, deeply in tune with the vibrations of the soil. The violinist, highly strung, would be the structural engineer. The architect the conductor."

In his book *A Vision of Britian* Prince Charles quotes Dr Fathi as pointing out that architecture for the poor should not be approached like the treatment of a special disease. He advocates an architecture that can be used by the rich and the poor alike:

> "Unfortunately, the poor are not given the advantage of aesthetics. People wrongly associate poverty with ugliness which is a mistake. The less expensive and poorer the project, the more care and attention that must be paid the aesthetics."

He goes on:

> "I say that beautiful architecture is an act of civility towards the person who comes into the building. It bows to you at every corner as in a minuet. Every ugly or senseless building is an insult to the man passing in front of it. Every building should be

embellishing and adding to its culture."

He asserts that this is very difficult to do now, because we have abandoned the human scale and the human reference. He suggests we need to re-introduce the human scale and musicality into architecture. He abhors the loss of craft skills, pointing out:

> "The revealed knowledge of the sage is now replaced by modern analytical science, while the skill of the craftsman's hand has been replaced by the machine."

Dr Fathi's remarkable life and work has shown us that it is possible to heal the destructive division between artists, craftsmen and architects whilst using local material and traditional skills in forms of building construction and use for materials which are energy efficient, aesthetically pleasing and of a sustainable form of construction. It highlights once again for us the importance of suiting our forms of science and technology, products and infrastructures to local and regional requirements. It highlights the importance of 'a sense of place'. The concept of products, skills and materials related to particular geographical areas will be of growing importance as we increasingly challenge the notion of the 'one best way'.

Throughout the world, there is now a growing recognition that this is so at many levels throughout society. I know from the response to my lectures, my writing and even to my television programmes, that there are many who can accept that what I say is relevant to a world of natural materials, craft skills, artistry integrated into processes or carried out in small-scale, cohesive communities. This they see as part of a world now gone and largely forgotten except in manifestations of the 'arty-crafty' case of wealthy elite minorities. They may accept that it finds some lingering expression in hand-made, customised shoes, clothes and odd pieces of furniture. They will even concede that it has some kind of lingering significance in the restoration of buildings and maybe modest architectural projects. What they find difficult to accept is that these ideas can be relevant in a world that has rapidly progressed to an information society.

I would object to this on two counts. Firstly, I do not accept that we live in an information society. We may live in a data society where data suitably selected and organised may become information. Information applied within a domain may become knowledge and knowledge absorbed within a culture may become wisdom. That wisdom may then lead to informed action.

Secondly, I believe that the ideas I have been advocating can have a pivotal relevance in the context of the new technologies. I was not alone amongst engineers and scientists in feeling that we could do better than design systems which reduced human beings to abject computer appendages. We noted with alarm that as the computer based systems became more powerful, so the human mind which had given rise to it was now being compared to the machine and in a manner which was increasingly derogatory. The brain began to be referred to as a 'meat machine' or slightly more generously as 'the only computer built by amateurs'. Human beings were increasingly asked to interact with machines in such a fashion, or to programme them in such a way that they gave of their intelligence to the machines. Their intelligence, which had been their bargaining power, their self image and esteem, had now been absorbed from them and embedded in computer programmes, relational databases, knowledge based systems, expert systems and intelligent controllers.

We had been assured that these advanced systems would be our slaves, but we quickly began to realise that the master/slave relationship was being reversed.

Fears and speculations about what might happen were suddenly transformed into stark reality. In some advanced computer controlled manufacturing systems, so active were the systems and so passive the human beings that technical journals began to point out that the ideal workers for such processes were mentally retarded workers. In one case cited by the *American Machinist*, a mental age of twelve was advocated. Had the objective been to provide work for the 'mentally retarded', this would of course have been laudable. What, however, we were witnessing was the destruction of the very seedbeds from which the future generations of skill and knowledge should come. As Professor Noble put it "If they are not mentally retarded when they go in, they will certainly be mentally retarded when they come out!"

Indeed this is so, for we need to think not merely of production but of the reproduction of knowledge. Where indeed will the next generations of skill and knowledge spring from if we deny human beings the capacity to continue to develop through their work?

We were indeed beginning to produce "Mr Zeros", so vividly predicted by Robert Boguslaw:

"Our immediate concern, let us remember, is the exploitation of the operating unit approach to systems design no matter what materials are used. We must take care to prevent this discussion from degenerating into the single-sided analysis of the complex characteristics of one type of systems material, namely human beings. What we need is an inventory of the manner in which human behaviour can be controlled, and a description of some of the instruments which will help us achieve that control. If this provides us with sufficient handles on human materials so that we can think of them as metal parts, electrical power or chemical reactions, then we have succeeded in placing human material on the same footing as any other material and can begin to proceed with our problems of systems design. There are, however, many disadvantages in the use of these human operating units. They are somewhat fragile, they are subject to fatigue, obsolescence, disease and even death. They are frequently stupid, unreliable and limited in memory capacity. But beyond all this, they sometimes seek to design their own circuitry. This in a material is unforgivable, and any system utilising them must devise appropriate safeguards."

We were being told that we need not think. Indeed, to think would simply constitute a systems disturbance. The era was already at hand in which machines would do our thinking for us.

CHAPTER 17

HUMAN CENTRED

In earlier chapters, I have described what I believe the long term consequences of such a development to be. I felt we had a responsibility to criticise such misguided design concepts and to demonstrate that it would be possible to design advanced computing systems in such a way as to utilise and enhance the most precious asset any society has which is the skill, ingenuity and creativity of its people.

Work commenced in the early '80s with my colleague Professor Rosenbrock at UMIST to develop a computer based system to control machine tools in such a way as to draw on the skill and knowledge of skilled workers rather than to marginalise their competence. We demonstrated that at the level of lathes and turning equipment. We were still confronted with the cynical approach which suggested that it may be possible to do this in respect of one machine but as systems moved through computerisation to integration, such a machine and its skilled operator would be an anachronism in the smooth flowing, reliable advanced integrated systems which covered all activities from design through production planning to manufacturing the end-product.

Our colleagues in Scandinavia had long been questioning the wisdom of this machine-based approach and interesting experiments at Volvo and the Utopia Project, supported by the Swedish Centre for the Quality of Working Life, showed that there was a willingness to explore alternatives to the given orthodoxy of machine-dependent systems.

Simultaneously in Germany where they had retained their skilled craft tradition, which was proving so successful in their economic development, they were approaching the same issue from a slightly different route known as Social Shaping. It was clear that funding bodies and multinational corporations were spending vast sums on systems which would lead to 'workerless factories'. From any research strategy viewpoint, it seemed most unwise to put all one's eggs in one basket. Furthermore, we took the view that funding bodies had a public responsibility to explore the potential of systems which would lay the basis for more satisfying and fulfilling work.

One of the potential advantages of the EEC is that it will have a market big enough, an economy strong enough, a culture diverse enough, and a tradition of research and development of sufficient flexibility to explore the possibilities of forms of science and technology and related product ranges which accord with the ecological, social, educational, cultural and historical expectations of the people of Europe. Furthermore, it could be a flexible technology which would reflect the rich mosaic of traditions and cultures that stretch across Europe from its windswept Celtic North West to its sunny Hellenic South East.

So it came about that in the early 80's a group of scientists, psychologists, social scientists, designers and industrialists from Britain, Denmark and Germany, came together in a most unusual multidisciplinary, multinational group.

As one of the initiators of the project, I and my colleagues approached Brussels unashamedly, to point out that we did not regard science and technology as objective and neutral but rather as part of culture. As such, since culture had produced different language, different literature and different music, we could not see why there should not be a different form of science and technology which reflected very different cultural and social implications. This approach laid the basis for a five million pound project to design and build that which we grandiosely referred to as the world's first human centred, computer integrated manufacturing system. It was less spectacularly known as Esprit Project 1217.

For those interested in the technical design details, my colleagues and I have produced a number of reports and books which cover those detailed aspects. I should like here to highlight only those aspects which relate to the general theme of this book.

The project built upon a tradition which I firstly described in 1976 as 'Human Centred'. We were aware from the onset, that to design a Human Centred System, we would have to challenge some of the sacred cows of the scientific methodology. Conventionally, a system is only regarded as being scientifically designed if it displays the three predominant characteristics of the natural sciences. That is to say, predictability, repeatability and quantifiability. That by definition precludes intuition, subjective judgement and tacit knowledge. It excludes imagination, emotion and, above all, the intentionality and purpose of the user.

Furthermore, we had realised that in the conventional form of systems design there is great concern to eliminate 'uncertainty'. In the design of such systems, the human being is seen as an uncertainty and an unpredictability and, therefore, good systems design includes the notion, if not stated explicitly, of marginalising human intelligence.

We set about questioning all of that and turning much of it on its head. We set about designing systems which would support human intelligence rather than marginalise it. In doing that, we were drawing on Heidegger's distinction between a tool and a machine. Heidegger would certainly not be my favourite philosopher, but he made the important distinction between a tool (*Zeug*) which would be "ready to hand or amenable" and a machine, which tends to act on the human being.

A tool supports the skill and ingenuity of the user and is amenable. In its best form and when it is in use, it is almost invisible and simply like an extension of ourselves. An analogy often used is that of the blind person with a white stick. As they tap along the edge of the pavement, they are conscious only of this edge and not of the white stick. In our work, powerful software tools were designed within this philosophy to support human intelligence.

Computers are now widely used to assist in the design process. On the screen, one can display and explore different design possibilities. It is easy to remove elements, substitute different ones, view the design from different angles and produce the final description of a component or the structure. At some stages in the design process it can be most helpful in calling up routine components and design data. What is noticeable however, is that designers frequently conceptualise their problems in forms which are compatible with the way the computer deals with them.

Furthermore, in many fields there have been developed optimised components and subsets. For example, in the design of a building there may be standardised doors, windows and much more that is standardised. In practice this means that the designer is really reduced to being like a child with a sophisticated lego set. They can make a pleasing pattern of predetermined elements but they can't change those elements. In the human centred approach, an innovative form of electronic sketchpad was developed by the Danish partners. It allows the designer to sketch any kind of element they wish. In other words, it restores to the designer the freedom of a renaissance artist.

The electronic sketchpad is portable and this means that one can take it around and have discussions with those who are going to make the components. In more advanced versions, the details of the proposed design could be sent electronically to the machines on the shop floor so that those who will ultimately make it can review what the designer is proposing and make suggestions as to how it might be improved. Whilst we prefer 'face to face' discussions using the sketchpad in its portable mode, there are circumstances where the electronic dialogue will also be useful. The views of many of those involved in making the product can thus be taken into account before the design is 'solidified'. This is restoring the interaction between the designer and the maker, a reuniting, as it were, of hand and brain.

For the production planning and scheduling sequences on the shop floor, the German partners have developed a workstation which can be used to render visible the advantages and disadvantages of different forms of scheduling components through the production procedures. It conveys a high level of transparency. That is to say it allows one to see easily what is going on in an otherwise complex situation. Their British counterparts at Human Centred Systems Ltd. have produced software so that you can display graphically the best way of planning production over several weeks.

These systems mean that the worker on the shop floor now becomes a cell manager, deciding on the spot how to optimise the production process. On the metal cutting machines themselves, the lathes for example, an interface has been designed which allows graphical programming. This accords much more with the tradional way in which skilled workers conceptualise a machining process and it draws upon and enhances their skill. There is displayed on the screen the blank piece of material which is going to be machined into a component. The skilled worker then envisages the best way of doing that and draws on the component, the form of the final object, using his imagination to conceptualise in advance what the component will be like.

This goes back to a very rich tradition of the 14th and 15th Century, when Michelangelo could say that he already saw the figure of David in the material before him, and that what he had to do was to remove all that which was not David. It's rather like that with this advanced machine interface.

The project is now being tested out in industry and, although much remains to be done, the results are already impressive. By using the system in a real manufacturing environment, Human Centred Systems Ltd. found there to be the following improvements: on-time delivery increased from 31% to 86%, manufacturing lead time was approximately halved, and work-in-progress reduced by 50%. Excess working hours to meet schedules was reduced by 75% so there are grounds for believing that even in the fields of advanced technology, alternative forms of design exist which can enhance rather than diminish human skill and, as with Dr Hassan Fathi's architecture, there is overall an enhanced use of human skill and creativity, more involvement of people, a better use of materials and a better product.

Central to this is the idea of human involvement and

commitment. A recent report from the United States, called ironically 'Made in America' but which was pointing out all the things they can no longer make there, asserted that the difficulties which are experienced in manufacturing arise at least in part from the fact that American industry has treated people as a liability, whereas in Germany and Japan people were treated as an asset whose skills should be ever enhanced.

Furthermore, there is now powerful evidence to show that if you have highly automated systems which include human intelligence, the systems are very vulnerable to disturbance. This occurs because it is highly synchronised and co-ordinated and, if one part of the system goes down, the high level co-ordination is suddenly turned into its opposite, almost in the sense of catastrophe theory. On the other hand, where there are skilled pro-active workers, they are capable of taking remedial steps and the resultant system is more flexible, robust and productive.

The principles of human centred systems which have been demonstrated in this ESPRIT project are now beginning to be applied more widely. New forms of learner technology (not teacher technology) have been developed in which there are audio, tactile and visual feedbacks. The systems are analogical rather than digital and provide for powerful simulation. It is somewhat equivalent in an engineering sense to flight simulators which pilots use to condense the learning time but of course, as with flying, it is only ultimately in practice that one can finally consolidate one's skill and know that one can really fly or act as a skilled worker in engineering.

In some of the more advanced proposals for learner technology innovative ways of using virtual reality are contemplated. In such systems a head-set is worn with a device which looks like a set of goggles and images are fed in as though one is seeing objects. A pair of gloves are worn which provide a sense of 'feel'. One can point in a particular direction and it is as though one is moving in that direction. It allows explorations of buildings yet to be constructed and layout of factories to be reviewed before the design steps have been finalised. As with computer aided design, virtual reality can be used either in a deskilling or enhancing mode.

Likewise, expert systems could be used in quite different ways. Many at the moment seek to capture the expertise of some professional and the system then issues decisions as to what should be done in certain circumstances. In many cases, the decisions of the expert are not rendered visible to the subsequent users and deskilling can thereby occur. Some of our work has laid the basis for systems which render visible the nature of the expert's decisions so that they can be queried and exploited.

Furthermore, in the case of medical expert systems, knowledge can be transmitted in such a way that the decisions of consultants and specialists in teaching hospitals can be diffused outwards so as to render visible to general practitioners the decisions of the consultants. This provides for a rich learning situation for the general practitioners but, more particularly in the surgery, the system displays different treatment options so that the patient and the medical practitioner are confronted with sets of options which means they must enter into a dialogue and one therefore builds democratising procedures into the system.

What is at the very core of all of this is whether we treat human beings as machines or accept their imagination, intentionality and commitment. As a result of the ESPRIT Project 1217 and arising from his other work, my colleague

Professor Howard Rosenbrock has written a book entitled *Machines with a Purpose*. In this, he questions the notion of a science based on causality and points out that in such a system one is inevitably forced to the conclusion that a human being is a machine. If, on the other hand, one viewed the human being as a system based on purpose, one would reach entirely different conclusions. So what all of these projects raise in a very direct way are the limitations experienced and the problems raised as a result of our own scientific methodology, and they are beginning to indicate fruitful alternatives we should explore.

The ideas set out above are as yet only discussed by a small number of academics and more sensitive employers who understand the ability of human commitment and involvement. They are questioning the whole basis of Taylorism. The Japanese have been doing so for some time. True their cultural background is very different from our own and as with all cultures it brings its strengths and weaknesses. But they have 'seen through' Taylorism and, as far back as 1979, Konosuke Matsushita jokingly chided visiting European Managers thus:

> "We are going to win and you in the industrial West are going to lose. There's nothing much you can do about it because the reasons for your failures are within yourselves. Your firms are built on the Taylor model. Even worse, so are your heads!"

So even in large business corporations, re-examination of the role of human beings is under way. Likewise, some of the more perceptive corporations are developing green audits of their products following some sharp prodding from environmental groups and green activists. Space is opening up for the ideas expressed in this book. The hope is that it will take place before irreversible damage has been done.

The EEC is likewise taking these ideas seriously. I chaired an EEC Expert Committee which produced a report titled *European Competitiveness in the 21st Century: The Integration of Work, Culture and Technology*. The report advocated Human Centred Systems (or anthropocentric as they are called in the EEC) and suggested long-life repairable, recyclable products. Above all, it emphasised the importance of diversity and pointed out that our society is rapidly going to have to move from an economy of scale to an economy of scope and then to an economy of networking.

At a more international level, the importance of these ideas is reflected in recognition through bodies such as the Right Livelihood Foundation or the Alternative Nobel Prize as it is known. Concerned at the way science, technology and development is damaging the planet, Jakob von Uexkull decided to sell his rare collection of stamps in order to lay the basis for a Nobel Prize for those whom he regarded as according more closely with the original values of Alfred Nobel when he said he wished to reward those who had best served humanity and made life more precious. Jakob von Uexkull offered to fund the additional prize for the Nobel Committee in 1979 and they rejected it. He then set up the Alternative Nobel Prize and now awards $100,000 each year to those who develop projects and systems which are sustainable and are replicable. Prizewinners drawn from science, the environmental movement and throughout the world include the Director of the Max Planck Institute in Munich and the leader of the Peruvian Indians.

There is then a growing recognition that we have lost our way and must explore those paths not taken; a recognition, as proposed by Amory and Hunter Lovins, that we must take personal responsibility for our role in these affairs. We must recognose that within your genes and mine is the legacy of thousands of millions of years of biological systems, evolving unbroken to the present day. Within your genes and mine is the heritage of all the children yet unborn, the potential for all time entrusted to our stewardship.

The omens are already ominous. As a species we have created a raven cloud:

> "...by the auspices of that raven cloud, your shade, and by the auguries of rooks in parliament, death with every disaster, the dynamitisation of colleagues, the reducing of records to ashes, the levelling of all customs by blazes, the return of a lot of sweetempered gunpowdered didst unto dudst."
>
> *James Joyce*

The raven clouds now gathering can engulf us all. Other species made themselves extinct by changing too slowly. It would be ironic if we as a species were to eliminate ourselves by changing too rapidly and in a manner which ignored our own humanity and our place in the natural world. Lest we forget, the planet is a stakeholder in all that we do!

We are a Cain and Abeled species, one tortuously twinned by Shem and Shaun, doctored by Jekyll and mutilated by Hyde in a society where the rampant Delinquent stalks the gentle Genius.

For a thousand years, the bellicose delinquent has conspicuously called the uneven odds, plundered the landscape, flattened the forests, oiled the cormorants, turned craftsmen into zombies, dignified Indians into reservation spectacles, the Aboriginal dreamtime into a nightmare, flowers into plastic, birds into battery hens, and the soil into a junkie crazed for its next fix.

The Delinquent instructs us that we are machines and should reside in factory cities, that our lives are soaps, our spirit an illusion, our humanity a liability, and our skills an uncertainty. He has Rambo'd our men, Bimbo'd our women, and zero'd our children. He insists on Oscar winning shows in the Gulf, Faustian performances at Chernobyl, and directs his own tragedies with Hitler and Stalin in the leading roles.

As the millennium draws precariously to its close, it still bears the Delinquent's stamp on every transaction. His face mocks and sneers at us from every hoarding. He is no longer incognito, invisible, submerged or implied. He now acts with open defiance of our every sensibility and is there for all to see. We shall have to number his days for time is not now on our side. His Ceausescu-like arrogance can now be his undoing. We must say that enough is enough and treat his attack on humanity's system as a form of historical vaccination.

The most fiendish ploy of the Delinquent has always been to chant the siren cry: "I am the one and only way". The 21st Century can and must belong to those who have the courage and common sense to reject this. Our future lies with those children, women and men who, in their very ordinary way, do care and can have within them, that long suppressed and extraordinary genius that resides in all of us and which now beckons us to heal our plagued planet and cure our disoriented selves.

INSULTING MACHINES

It is a graceful degradation, bristling with paths not taken
Supercharged by Taylor's one best way
with all the zeal of the monotheist
Where Schumpeter shoves, Kondratiev waves and Gladwell points
All in hot pursuit of singularity.
Behold the strange phyla as they stalk their makers
They too can walk, feed, talk and – some say – think.

We create devices and then they create us.
Narcissus-like, we gaze into a pool of technology and see ourselves.
We acquiesce in our own demise, setting out as participants
and metamorphosing into victims.
The diagnosis is serious: a rapidly spreading species' loss of nerve
Tacit knowledge is demeaned whilst propositional knowledge is revered.
Who needs imagination when there are facts?

A human enhancing symbiosis ignored
whilst a dangerous convergence proceeds apace – as human beings
confer life on machines and in so doing diminish themselves.

Your calculus may be greater than his calculus
but will it pass the Sullenberger Hudson River test?
Meantime, the virtual is confused with the real
 – as parents lavish attention on the virtual child
whilst their real child dies of neglect and starvation.

Potential and reality are torn apart as change is confused with progress
With slender knowledge of deep subjects
 – you proceed with present tense technology,
obliterating the past and with the future already mortgaged.
The court of history may find you intoxicated with species arrogance
recklessly proceeding without a Hippocratic Oath.

Meantime, the deskiller is deskilled, as a tsunami of technology
rocks our foundations.
The multinational apologist solemnly declares "We should have the
courage to accept our true place in the evolutionary hierarchy
– namely animals, humans and post singularity systems".
Now the sky darkens with pigeons coming home to roost
and the mine canaries topple from their perches unnoticed.

That distant sound grows louder.
Is it the life affirming energy of Riverdance
or the clacking hooves of the Four Horsemen?
That music, is it 'Ode to Joy' or is it 'Twilight of the Gods?'
As the embrace tightens into genteel strangulation – will the seducer
in final deception whisper "Shall I compare thee to a Summer's day?"

Mike Cooley

This poem was first published in AI & Society *Vol.28 No.4 Dec 2013*

SOURCES

"I am a part of all that I have met;
Yet all experience is an arch wherethro'
Gleams that unravell'd world, whose margin fades
For ever and forever when I move."

Ulysses, Tennyson

I have a quite good memory which on occasion is even mildly Mozartian. It is however suspect in at least one respect: it is notoriously selective. This, I like to tell myself, is a bad habit acquired through the practice of a good one – that of emphasising the positive.

I recall the glass of circumstance to have been half full whilst many contemporaries and observers may perceive it to have been half empty. I do not mean patently ridiculous positivism but, rather, a creative view of what can be achieved with the materials to hand rather than an extended exposition of what cannot be undertaken. The former involves a 'can do' as well as a 'can analyse' mentality. Problems are fascinating in the sense that, if creatively handled, they will usually yield up their own solutions. Delightfully 'wicked' problems do not admit to one elegant solution and their solution usually involves a subtle mix of trade-offs.

I have always enjoyed attempting to solve problems rather than merely intellectualising them. In consequence, I tend to view circumstances for what they might become rather than what they are at present – in somewhat the way a craftsman may think of an elegant chair when looking at a rough plank of hardwood.

This outlook usually provokes the accusation of being non-analytical, uncritical and unrealistic. However, like the Berkeley students in the 60's, I keep advising myself "Don't adjust your mind, there's a fault in reality". My expectations of my childhood and education were quite unrealistic. My selective memory recalls that those expectations were usually fulfilled.

My life has been made up of unlikely 'can do' or at least 'can try' projects which led to constructive outcomes. They make me what I am, how I think and what I feel. It is these events and circumstances that I recall, the things that went right rather than the things that went wrong or the infinity of steps which if taken, might have gone wrong. I do abhor the destructive barbarism of negative recollection and though like a craftsman I may illustrate that which won't work, like them I emphasise and hand on that which will work.

My childhood worked for me. I claim no more for it than that. It required no great insight on my part to see that others, some of them more intelligent than myself and in similar circumstances, just about managed. Others seemed to just sink without trace. I believe I thrived.

It occurred to me at an early stage that it's not just circumstance but also how one reacts to it that determines outcomes. I positively relished the excitement of a 'pick-and-mix' comparatively simple but holistic upbringing. I had a gifted childhood. It scintillated with all those marvellous activities and exciting escapades which are conventionally regarded as suspect and diversionary. It was unstructured, diverse, close to nature, chaotic, sometimes downright dangerous and nearly always great fun. It was holistic in a manner modern society no longer tolerates and which progress has now exorcised.

I was born in 1934 into a small business family and we were, at least in a relative sense, reasonably well off. This had of course some significance, but it was really the circumstance of time and place that moulded my life.

I grew up in a small town in the West of Ireland called Tuam. With its five thousand citizens, it was large enough to provide for diversity but not so large as to be overwhelming. It was to be the grain of sand in which I would see the whole world.

My earliest recollections are of warmth. That delightful yin and yang sensation of a warm bed in a cold room. The horizons expanded and I became intrigued with one source of warmth – the fireplace. Firemaking is one of the key technological skills that enabled our species to transcend the "Jungle VIP". It is deeply rooted in the collective consciousness of our species. I vividly recall the psychological and physical comfort of sitting round a peat or log fire and internalising that extraordinary ability of humans to transform materials into heat energy. The logs spluttered and crackled in protest whilst flames like dragon tongues caressed them into lifeless ashes.

Lifting small logs from the stack to feed the greedy fire gave me a good sense of how much material had to be used up to provide us with a modest heat. I had also witnessed the backbreaking work of crosscutting those logs and extracting the peat (turf) from the bogs. I have never since taken heat and energy for granted.

Tuam at that time was still primitive enough for young people to experience the pleasure and education of an open fire. In most houses the fire was used for the cooking as well. But socially, the fire had a wider significance. Because we were still backward enough for people to wish to talk to each other, there was a rich storytelling tradition. Around a fireplace one could feel the collective consciousness of our cave dwelling past. Against the dark unlit background of the room, the fire frontlighted an array of Rembrandt heads and hands.

Often, a concert of human voices would recount in turn the ancient folk tales of the West of Ireland. They would recede into a chilling whisper or build to a crescendo as they described the near factual crossing of a stormy sea. There was instilled at that early formative stage a love of language and the spoken word which still permeates the best of Irish theatre.

Our family home was on top of a hill on the edge of the town. Beyond our house lay 'the country'. This was the gentle, windswept, boggy, marshy, limestone landscape of North Galway. I had at my back door a treasure trove of flora and fauna. The location of our house qualified me by about 100 yards as a 'town child'. This seemed to be regarded as more desirable than being a 'country child'.

Our home was by comparison a modern one. We had electric light. In that area and at that time, electricity was the new technology. We were really in a phase of transition. The network of pylons and supply lines was somewhat fragile and the supply not entirely reliable. We therefore retained some of the old technology (paraffin oil lamps) just in case.

In winter, the West coast of Ireland is swept by ferocious storms. Trees would be uprooted, supply lines fell and the force of nature would plunge us into sudden darkness. As a small child, I recall the excitement of then lighting the paraffin lamps. The electric light was bright, harsh and consistent if it was on at all. It was there at the flick of a switch. There was no coaxing it and my parents only knew how much they had used when the bill arrived.

The lamps were different. It was a transparent technology on a human scale. We could see what fuel we were using. When the bulbous base was filled with the oil, I could adjust the wick level with a drive mechanism to make a low or high flame and I could make it smoke or flicker. I was always fascinated with the way the wick tape functioned. I was intrigued that the liquid should move upwards along the tape whereas my tea always travelled down my spoon! Reading was of course more difficult with the oil lamp and my mother would have to hold her needlework close to it to discern the pattern of her work. It obviously had deep disadvantages as I noted from my school friends who lived 'down the country' and for whom it was the only source of lighting.

My mother's analogy of the oil climbing the wick with the moisture climbing the stem of a plant didn't satisfy. It didn't describe the mechanism. My childish imagination was aflame with possibilities for this.

Was the paraffin made up of lots of little insect-like creatures that could climb up the wick of the lamp but could not climb the spoon because it was too slippery? Were there lots of little red creatures at the end of the poker that could climb up along it with fewer and fewer of them making the long journey to the end? The fascination which these questions inspired in me then burns as vividly today even if it is now in a much more sophisticated form.

I often helped my school friends in the country to draw water from the well. I remember as a six or seven year old, helping to carry buckets of water from the well as the sharp rim of the handle bit into my hands on the 200 yard journey back to their house. In contrast, we were connected to the mains. In our home, we turned a tap and the water was there. That seemed to me to be a great achievement and it still does today. We flushed a toilet and more water went in one go than the amount I had carried in the laborious journey from the well. That seemed to me to be wasteful then and it still does now.

The well from which we drew the water had an almost mystical quality. Its water was marvellously clear and clean and even on the warmest summers day was refreshingly cool. I learned in that simple way to appreciate the value of a clear, clean supply of water and I have never since taken it for granted. It was as though my childhood was preparing me for that stage we are now approaching where our technologically advanced societies can no longer guarantee us an adequate supply of this clear, clean water and the supply to many US cities is now precariously short.

Our family business was only a couple of hundred yards from our house. It included a garage and an engineering workshop. When my mother went into the town shopping, I would be sometimes left in my father's care in the workshop. I used to sit in some kind of small chair with wheels which my father would bring around to the point where he was working so that he could talk to me and I could see some of the activity. Most fascinating was when they were brazing metal parts together. The basic pieces of metal would be heated and spelter would be added as small solid pieces of metal which dissolved into a liquid as they touched the hot surface. A flux would be added and an eerie greenish blue flame would emerge as it bubbled and spluttered on the surface. When the materials cooled down they would be solidly bonded together.

My imagination raved as to what could be happening.

Why did the spelter turn to liquid? How did the materials link together after the process? Could it have been that some of the little creatures that ran along the poker in the fire at home also used to run along these materials, and run from one material to another, and then somehow grip together, moulding them together solid?

I remember well when I was about four or five, my father showing me that if you attempt to hammer a piece of metal when it was cold it would hardly change form at all, but if you hammered it when it was red hot, the metal would 'flow' as he put it. I wondered if, when the material was cold, the little creatures gripped strongly to each other, whereas when it was hot their grip was weaker and the hammer blows could more easily spread them apart. Other materials, I realised, behaved quite differently.

At home, as my mother made delicious apple cakes, she would let me make my own small cake alongside. I noticed to my amazement that the little patterns on the top of the soft dough, when cooked, changed from being soft to being solid and crisp; completely the opposite of what happened to the metal in my father's workshop. My imaginary little creatures in this material, for some reason, behaved in the opposite way to those in the metal. These ones gripped more closely together when they were heated.

During the long dark winter evenings my mother would read a lot to us or tell us fascinating stories. I learned my alphabet at home and could soon recognise some small words which my mother would point out in the midst of some fascinating story. I didn't start school until I was seven and when I did it seemed somewhat of a diversion from all the interesting things I was doing. My primary school was the Presentation Convent in Tuam. I enjoyed learning to read and write but always ensured that I called in to my father's workshop on the way home and spent quite a lot of time there on Saturdays.

I now realise that at that early stage I loved to conceptualise things and explain them as analogies. This took quite an unexpected and quantum step forward during my first or second year at school. Our education was religious and Catholic. One of the advantages amongst (as many would point out) the host of disadvantages is that a religious upbringing causes you to think of matters and processes external to yourself and which transcend your immediate environment. I used to speculate with my little school friends what heaven and hell were really like.

Early on in our religious instruction, we were told that heaven (or for that matter, hell) would go on for all eternity. I must have been about eight then and I could not really find a framework in which to conceptualise eternity. There was a nun in the convent whose name I believe was Sister Furzey. I asked her about this and she said eternity really meant a very, very long time; so long that it just went on for ever.

This I found quite unsatisfactory. I had seen plants grow and die. I had seen my grandmother die and I simply could not get a sense of the scale of eternity so I pursued this with Sister Furzey and I always recall that as we stood in the grounds of the Presentation Convent, she pointed across to the huge cathedral which was about 150 yards away and said: "If you imagine that that huge building is made of the hardest metal and every 100 years a wagtail flies by and just touches it with its tail, well eternity would be something like how long it would take to wear away". She explained also that 100 years was a bit longer than my granny's lifetime. It was powerful imagery.

In winter, the field at the back of our house was an ornithologists delight. On those dark November afternoons, when powerful West winds seemed to drive the rain horizontal to the ground, golden plover, grey plover, green plover, curlews and a wide variety of seagulls all came within some ten yards of our back wall. Crouched in a shelter I would observe them through a gap for literally hours on end. It seemed they were putting on a performance specially for me.

The evening flight of the lapwing was the most spectacular but for an embryonic aerospace engineer, the almost motionless hovering of seagulls in these powerful winds was a provocation one could not resist. I failed to see why if they could do it, I – properly equipped – could not do likewise. So inspired by seagulls and equipped with a childish sense of engineering, I decided at nine to fly. Various forms of wings were constructed and tested. The preferred solution was a frame constructed like a bow with its arrow fixed in position. Sheets of the Irish Independent newspaper were then used for purposes for which they were certainly not intended and patently not suited. Sheets were placed on either side of the frame and stuck together with a home made adhesive of flour and water. The end result looked quite presentable. It even seemed robust compared with the wings of a butterfly, which I had observed disintegrate even at a gentle touch.

I decided I would launch myself from the top of the Protestant Bishop's Palace wall. It was just across from our house, was relatively easy to climb and was wide enough at the top to give me a sound footing from which to launch myself.

One of my great confidants was Mr Higgins, a neighbour in his 70s, who used to talk to me for hours and never seemed to tire of listening to my various schemes. He would also tell me what life was like "in the old days". We would sit at the side of the road chatting whilst he steadied himself with his ancient stick, gripped with his delicate sensitive hands that were a whitish yellowy colour, and when the sun shone on them appeared translucent like candles. We spoke for hours about the wings of different species and the manner of flight. He never said my scheme was reckless or stupid when I announced that on the next really windy day, I would launch myself from the Palace wall. He said: "Don't be disappointed if you don't get far from there". I often wondered if this was a technical assessment or an expression of religious doubt about my launchpad.

One of my school friends was an untiring assistant in my experiments. He would faithfully carry out my suggestions at the preparatory stages, but never actually participate in the experiment as such. On the stormy November day of the launch in what seemed to me to be an act of considerable disbelief, he gathered a huge pile of leaves vertically below my launchpad. He peered up at me and said "It's just in case". He became a schoolteacher, now a head teacher, and I became an engineer.

Then as an unselfconscious successor of Icarus, I started to flap my wings, shouted "I'm flying", jumped forward and crashed down vertically into the leaves. "I did fly a little didn't I?" I asked him and he obligingly said "Oh you did, you really did" and by way of qualification added "but only a little bit".

My little universe was a whirlwind of activities and engagements. I loved to rough shoot with my father. I had a mental map of all the best locations for snipe, pigeon, woodcock and, during the winter, the geese. I read avidly about their navigational activities and never tired of discussing with sportsmen their characteristics and traits. I had a great respect for the species we pursued and learned to know and respect their habitat and participate in their conservation.

Some of the birds we came to know individually. There was a huge cock pheasant in Gardenfield Wood, and when a local sportsman firstly told me about him and described where I might catch a glimpse of him, I asked if he was a large bird. With a beautiful analogy he said: "God if he'd riding breeches on you'd think he was Malachy O'Keefe himself!"

There were great fishermen in the town. Some could make up their own split cane rods and all of them could tie a myriad of different flies, sometimes using feathers which we provided from the game birds. Year in, year out they pursued a huge trout that lurked in the dark pools of the local river to erupt from its depths on a summer evening, with a spectacular rise and related splash. Tom Pierce had tied a particularly spectacular fly which he showed me as he set out to pursue the trout. I asked him how he would feel if he succeeded in catching it. It would be a great disappointment to both of us, evoking the intimate but ambivalent nature of the hunter and the hunted as only a North American Indian could understand it. Was this sustainable relationship to be ruthlessly ruptured by modern techniques which can pinpoint a single fish at a depth of five hundred metres?

By the time I went to the Christian Brothers Secondary School there never seemed to be enough hours in the day to allow me to do all the things I wanted to do.

My favourite subject was geometry and I used to spend hours at home working out alternative constructions. Biology was exciting because it widened my understanding of the species I had come to know and understand through interacting with them. Afternoons and weekends I would work in my father's garage and workshop. By the time I was 13 or 14 I had already acquired rudimentary diagnostic skills and could time two-stroke and four-stroke engines. I rebuilt from scratch an old motor cycle.

The town had a number of small amateur theatre groups and I would avidly attend their performances. The highlight was when Emma McMaster's Shakespearian Theatre Group would visit the town. They would perform in the town hall in the square and even if one did not understand it all, the spectacular nature of the performances compensated for any lack of detailed comprehension of the themes involved. Above all, there was the sound of the human voice as it emerged into the small, dark streets which led on to the square.

At school I enjoyed languages enormously, even Latin. Although German was not taught at our school, it had somehow fired my imagination from an early age. On the one hand in the cinema, there was portrayed on occasion the hysterical shouting of Hitler and I wondered what anybody could say that would move so many people to such hideous lengths. I contrasted this with the beautiful, evocative and analogical descriptiveness of some German poems I found in a book of "foreign poetry". As I returned from school one day, a lorry stopped on the high street loaded with pieces of machinery for the workshops of the sugar factory. Through the crate I eagerly perused all the extraordinary foreign words. On a grinding machine I noticed an amazing word – *Schleifscheibedortmesser*. I determined there and then that a language which produced words of such glorious length and undoubtedly wondrous sounds used by both Hitler and

Heine must be explored more deeply.

The head of the engineering workshops was one Franz Kaplan. He lived with his wife on the Ballygaddy Road. Given that there were no other possible ways of learning German that I could think of, I decided on a bold approach. One afternoon I simply went to the Kaplan's home and knocked. When the rather sedate and very Viennese Mrs Kaplan emerged, I clearly startled her by announcing that I had come to learn German. No amount of reasonable explanation about how difficult it would be and the time it would take mattered at all. I told her with childlike directness that I wanted to know which days I could come so that she could speak German to me and I assured her that I would learn it in no time! Two years later I could speak German quite fluently and could read straightforward articles in German newspapers. I always point out I learned German rather than studied it.

In parallel with this, I was very keen to learn technical drawing. The subject was not given in the Christian Brothers school but it was available at the local technical school. The technical school was for those who would pursue practical vocational careers and was seen as the place where those who couldn't do any better would end up. On the other hand it seemed to me to present enormous potential.

Tuam in 1949/50 was certainly not the centre of comprehensive education, indeed the notion hadn't caught on to any great extent in England or elsewhere, so my scheme was rather bold by any standards. I proposed to attend both schools and thereby get the selection of subjects I desired. This caused sheer consternation in the Christian Brothers school and my class tutor, Brother Rafferty, explained to me with obvious concern for my future that the only children who went to "that place" were the children from Gilmartin Road (this was a working class part of the town). He predicted that it would finish me and that, in any case, it was not possible to have pupils attending two schools even if the timetable could be arranged.

I was still determined to pursue these technical subjects which did require equipment and facilities I couldn't obtain elsewhere. I persuaded my parents to allow me to leave the Christian Brothers school and go to what was disparagingly called "The Tech". My strategy was to pursue my languages, literature and arts subjects more generally outside school and to concentrate on the more technical and vocational subjects during the school day. It worked out admirably. At the tech there was a very committed arts teacher, Miss Butler, who used to even organise for travelling painting exhibitions to take place in the tech. I developed an interest in painting in a somewhat craft tradition rather than in an expressionist form. I attempted landscapes in both watercolour and oil. The real influence there was a gifted metalwork teacher called Sean Cleary.

School was for me, therefore, just one of many educational influences in a context which was balanced by the practical engineering activities of my father's workshop and a host of recreational and social activities which were so enriching and absorbing that I could never understand how friends my own age, growing up at the same time and from the same background, used to profess to be "bored".

I could see, during my years from 16 to 18, that to pursue my interests further, particularly in a higher educational context, would mean that I would have to concentrate more narrowly and abandon the holistic environment which I enjoyed so enormously. I particularly resented the notion that I might have to give up languages and concentrate just on engineering and vice versa, when I loved both.

Whilst making up my mind how to resolve this dilemma, I decided to absorb as much knowledge of engineering as I could and entered the local sugar factory as an apprentice whilst I thought through the best way to handle the destructive options which society seemed to present. I could not accept or understand that it was not possible to be a good engineer and a committed linguist at the same time.

The few short months spent in the sugar factory were incredibly enriching. I had the opportunity of working with skilled craftsmen on the overhaul of steam turbines, big Diesel generating sets and a range of machine tools which I had never previously encountered. I realised too that the craftsmen had different and complementary skills and I would deliberately seek them out in turn so as to absorb as much from them as I could. I discussed with Franz Kaplan, who was head of the workshops, the dilemma about language and engineering and he suggested an elegant solution. Why not study engineering in a German speaking country? This is precisely what I then set about doing.

This yin and yang approach worked out admirably. There followed in Germany and Switzerland study and qualifications in engineering and technology. In parallel was a deepening knowledge of German language, literature and theatre. It was a form of learning by emotion, a kind of intellectual osmosis. I delighted in the regional variations of the language, each with their distinctive meaning, significance and nuance of a Babylon within a Babylon. My rendering of Schweizerdeutsch, which I picked up whilst working at Machinenfabrik Oerlikon, is still convincing.

Cultural opportunities seemed to multiply exponentially. In a cultural multiplier effect one could listen to some of Europe's finest orchestras, hear Goethe in the original and see the archives of Dürer. Zurich was ideal geographically for Northward trips to the South German cities, Eastwards to Vienna and the old central Europe, and, with breathtaking revelation, journeys to the South and the Tuscan city states. These were indeed my "Wanderjahre".

None of this diminished my sheer delight in engineering and science. It actually enhanced it. At Machinenfabrik Oerlikon I worked on powerful steam and gas turbines, power units for locomotives, generators for power stations and even on a girobus. This was the same beloved engineering of my father's workshop, but now on a scale and in a form which appeared to diminish me and threaten nature. A photograph I still possess shows me as a minute figure standing on one of the giant flanges of a huge generating set. I had my first doubts then that this could go on and go on.

I moved to London to work on missile design. Even in the late 50's their guidance systems were beginning to be awesomely accurate, the forerunners of the Gulf surgical strikes. It was breathtaking engineering, but of awesome implications. When I moved temporarily to work on "peaceful projects" with a Swedish company designing huge water turbines for vast hydro schemes, I realised that they too were not without their implications. The dams in which they would be located would flood valleys and terrains for miles around.

In the design of the systems we came increasingly to use computers. They were then just number crunchers but already we were starting to conceptualise our problems in forms which were compatible with the computers. There followed my PhD in Computer Aided Design, in which I questioned some of the inbuilt values in these apparently neutral activities.

I was working at the time in the aerospace industry and I have recounted elsewhere the Plan for Socially Useful Production. Simultaneously, there followed Guest Professorships, mainly in Germany, and then subsequently in the United States and Japan.

There was a wealth of unselfconscious artist/crafts people in Tuam. Their true artistry was concealed behind deceptively simple *noms de plume*. The blacksmith would design art metalwork by sketching with his poker on the floor of his forge. Decorative gates bedecked with intricate vines, building enhancing railings and spiral staircases that invited ascension, were all coaxed into form by the knowing blows of his hammer. The cobbler at the bottom of "our hill" could design and make from scratch anything from unpretentious, honest boots, through dress shoes, to full length riding boots, all hand stitched and all guaranteed as she put it "to fit like a glove". A young woman from Galway almost apologetically displayed the skill absorbed from her old mother. "Sure it's nothing really", she'd say, "I made up the pattern in my head before I started" as she defensively produced an intricately designed hand woven Claddagh shawl.

Perhaps it was my brash precociousness, but to me it seemed they enjoyed endlessly chatting to me whilst they continued their work. Craftspeople continue to work as they talk. Intellectuals have to stop to make the explanation more profound. Each craft workplace had its own ambience, smell and atmosphere which seemed integral to the skills deployed. The craft would be described to me by simple analogy and evocative demonstration: "I do it like this". I was already beginning to get an inkling of the terrible confusion in our society between linguistic ability and intelligence.

For me, the pinnacle of these artist/crafts people were those casually referred to as stone cutters. They were in fact sculptors and master stone masons of a very high standard.

When my grandmother died I accompanied my father when he went to discuss the sculpting of a gravestone with the stonecutter on the Old Road. His workshop was really an open yard, part of which was covered with a galvanised roof. He worked in primitive conditions with simple tools and produced work of extraordinary beauty. We walked round the little yard and he pointed out the different stone that might be used, briefly describing the characteristics, advantages and drawbacks of each type and the relative cost. His ability to elicit from my father the kind of monument he required, and then feed it back to him as a set of proposals was astonishing. "Would you like a cross?" he started. Had my father said "yes" he would have described the different types starting perhaps with Celtic-type crosses decorated with zoomorphic motifs. My father said he didn't really want a cross. He had in mind a figure of some kind.

The imagination flowed as the stonecutter enquired whether Christ with a crown of thorns, or a mother and child might be appropriate. A quick process of elimination homed in on an angel. Would he like the angel looking down sadly upon the grave or perhaps looking up towards heaven, which he demonstrated by holding his hands as in prayer and looking upwards at an angle. Did he wish to have the wings outstretched? Simple sketches were used to indicate the base on which it might stand.

Within ten or fifteen minutes, a clear mutual understanding had emerged on what the figure would be like, what material would be used and how much it would cost, yet no written tender existed, no material specification and, above all, no drawing or any dimensions other than the understanding that the angel would be "about as big as myself". As we left, the stonecutter said to me: "If you call in next week, I'll show you the slab".

The slab, when it arrived, was laid out horizontally on two huge chunks of wood. He showed me the grain of the material and described its strengths and weakness. The neck of the figure would be the weak point and this determined which end of the slab would be the base.

In the days that followed, he would tell me to return on a given day when, as he put it: "The head will be coming out". It was as though it were being born out of the stone. He showed me the point at which the hands would emerge and when they did, the beautifully shaped fingers were interlaced in prayer set off by slender wrists, which emerged from draped sleeves of a flowing gown whose folds were so realistically executed that one might expect to see them move in a gentle wind. He had learned his craft from his father and uncle. Like Michelangelo, who was probably unknown to him, he could see the figure of the angel in the raw material and all he was doing was removing all that was not the angel. It was then revealed in all its glory.

My mind boggled then and still boggles today as to the extraordinary sense of shape, size and form so unpretentiously displayed by these craftspeople. I was later to see people get degrees in fine art in London and elsewhere whose abilities it seemed to me were trivial compared with those displayed in this small underdeveloped town. Yet it was already clear to me as a child that the emerging educational structures were insensitive to this kind of knowledge and would ignore it or bring about its demise.

When I discuss those early years in Tuam, it is sometimes suggested that I take a romantic view. I disagree. What I did then and what I do to this day is always to emphasise the positive. Problems on the other hand I see as situations in need of a solution. I believe the definition of a problem should be in a form which indicates a solution. There were of course many problems in Tuam at that time. Whilst my personal circumstances protected me from them, I was deeply aware of their existence.

There was abject poverty in some parts of the town. At my first school children turned up on bitter winter days shivering and hungry with skinny chilblained legs, ragged dirty clothes and runny noses. I was deeply shocked when a child who had been watching me eat my packed lunch made the bizarre offer that he would drink my bottle of ink or eat a live spider or a cockroach if I would give him one of my biscuits. These were also the children that bullying teachers would pick on because they realised they had no one to speak for them. I could see at an early stage that the meek were not about to inherit the earth.

My mother, one of the Brownes of Galway, had a sharp social conscience and abhorred injustice in any form. She was engaged in several charitable and voluntary activities. She disliked and ridiculed the hierarchal structure of the town which she described as "A ha'penny looking down on a farthing". She could be ferocious in her defence of the underdog. A shock wave ran through the town when it was learned that a child from the poorer part of the town had committed suicide. He had been accused of taking a few pennies from the shop where he ran errands on a Saturday to supplement the family's meagre existence. The Garda (police) had taken him into the police station on his own and held him for several hours of questioning. He was released in a distraught state, went to the shop, opened the "poison cupboard" and took a lethal dose. He died in terrible pain.

When news of this reached my mother, she was furious.

She fixed her brown hat particularly firmly on her head, took me by the hand and stormed up the high street to the police station. With no direct evidence whatsoever but with an acute sense of circumstantial injustice, she told the alarmed and speechless sergeant that the police were responsible for the child's death. "You wouldn't have held the bank manager's son or my son on their own and treated them in that way." And then like a high court judge summed up "You're a disgrace to your uniform in a country that is supposed to cherish all its people equally. If I find out which of you is responsible for this crime, I'll see that he spends the rest of his days in Mountjoy" (prison). These were the sort of lessons one seldom learns at school.

I sensed that the disadvantaged needed to organise themselves and my later interest in the positive aspects of trade unionism was sparked at that early stage.

The houses in the poorer part of town were often dilapidated, and unhygienic – a downright health hazard. I could see at first hand how simple technology, plumbing, sewage, effective heating could transform their lives. I realised that health depended as much on engineering as it did on medicine. I was never depressed by such sights, nor did I see any point in whingeing about them. My approach has always been and continues to be "let's do something about it".

The cinema had a great impact on all of us. These were Laurel and Hardy days as we mimicked their every gesture in an impersonation which always ended with the inevitable "That's another fine mess you got me into Stanley". Those with more earnest dramatic ambitions gave chilling renderings of Peter Lorre, accent, sad eyes and all. The cinema was a great source of information and, in equal measure, of misinformation. It took me years to dislodge the nonsense it instilled about the American Indians.

Equally compelling to the professional theatre was our own, rather absurd amateur one. My father had a hand operated cinematograph which showed silent films. It would be ceremoniously taken out on Christmas nights. The speed at which the handle rotated determined whether the frames were absurdly 'jerky' or projected in a reasonably fluent movement.

My brother and I found a way of driving the films backwards. It was fascinating. People emerged from rivers, shot upwards and ended up standing on the edge of a bridge. I was fascinated that one could reverse processes of this kind, but hardly anything in the real world could be reversed. The baby chick could not be put back in the egg. I became intrigued with what was reversible and what was non-reversible. I also thought it strange that if the screen was the receiver of the image, it required no energy to receive whereas our radio did require an electrical supply. In my father's garage we used to charge the lead/acid batteries for the local farmers so that they could connect them up to their radios. With the cinema, it appeared that the energy was required to transmit the signal outwards but the receiver did not require enery. With the radio, energy was required both to transmit and receive the signal.

In many ways I preferred the radio to the cinema because it left more scope for imagination. Our whole family used to sit round to listen to the Sunday night play. The imagination was hyperactive, locating the voices in some kind of imaginary context.

During the week we listened to 'Dick Barton Special Agent'. I could imagine the veins standing out on Jock's throat as he was locked in mortal combat with some terrible baddie.

Our radio had a round dial with the names of the cities throughout the world. Each had an associated number but I preferred the names and would look them up on the atlas and imagine what each of them looked like. It seemed so much more vivid than thinking just of a wavelength as on a modern dial.

I was amazed to notice on an atlas that the stations furthest away were to be found on the short waveband whereas those closer were generally transmitted on the long wave. At a simple level this seemed wrong and stimulated an interest in finding out the significance of wave frequencies.

Although of course there were moments of disappointment and frustration and anger, in an overall sense I was conscious of being deeply happy and feeling lucky to be alive at that place and time. All around me seemed alive: the fields, the trees, the skies, the rivers and I felt myself to be completely a part of nature itself, continuously interacting with it and learning from it. It seemed to me that to damage nature would be like damaging myself.

I used actually to listen to nature. It was an exhilarating feeling when I was out night shooting with my father, to hear all the sounds of nature and the wind in the dark. I feel sorry for children whose education has not allowed them those sensations.

The motor cycle I rebuilt had been rescued from a barn where its old chrome plated tank was just about visible through some straw. Its cylinders were lovingly bored, its valves reground, new bearings fitted and it purred like new when rebuilding was complete. It was already clear that great possibilities existed for truly repairable and ultimately recyclable products but that required sets of skills which were rapidly in retreat.

A GRAND TOUR

Images of Craft Skills in 1940s Tuam

It was a place of unselfconscious artists/craftspeople
whose embodied knowledge is that marvel, human
skill
which causes inert tools to spring into life as biddable
extensions of the knowing hand, producing art concealed as work which always revealed the hand of the
maker.
Where tools and materials supported those, skilled with
talents fine-tuned over centuries
and whose tacit knowledge and sense of quality
lurked in unpretentious work spaces.
Artefacts hidden in the guise of the ordinary so
familiar as to be unnoticed.
For we see but little of what is there and find instead,
merely what we seek.
This then was the setting for a grand tour in a small
place,
guided only by the tutor of his intrusive curiosity in
this, his Florence on the Nanny,
a treasure trove of much used but little appreciated artefacts.
Now on a drizzly October day he would embark upon
his initial Wanderjahre
by going nowhere special — for the greatest journeys
are always in the mind.

Perched halfway down the Tullinadaly hill,
stood the workshop of Henry Creighton & Son – coach
builders.
The huge sliding front doors, like the curtains in a
theatre,
slid back to reveal the cavernous workshop behind.
A hand-made side car nearing completion, where

father coached son as his father had done. Then
armed only with a spokeshave, blocks of wood were
transformed
into delicate, graceful wheel spokes like the limbs of
a ballet dancer.
At the back, their very own ring of fire where the heat
expanded the wheel rim
so that it fitted snugly and tightened the wheel as it
contracted.
Fitted to a well greased axle, soon to take the Lyns-
key family into town on Sundays
If Jarlath's chariot had a Creighton wheel, where
might Tuam be today?

A stone's roll downhill, almost unnoticed —
hid the tiny snug leather-scented workshop of shoe-
maker Doris Hosty.
The shoe-last in the window, a symbol and a tool with
paraffin lamp of eye damaging inadequacy
where handmade shoes seemed to grow from the
materials spread on a small work surface
while throughout the town there was no shortage of
those to testify
that the shoes she made would fit like a glove, put a
spring in your step and last for years.
One proud owner known for hyperbola, asserted that
any self respecting corpse
would be proud to be laid out in them.

Now, meandering along the Old gardens pathway to
the Old Road where the Rooney brothers
sculpted beneath the galvanised roof of their windswept workspace.
There they 'liberated' Angels or Celtic Crosses as if
by magic
from the pregnant stone in which they could already

see the figure
and would remove 'all that was not David' until he
emerged resplendent.
Then the hand eye and brain combined to direct the
spectacular chisel movements
And beneath its cutting edge, beauty was manifest.
Yet these artist craftspeople were kept 'below the
salt' by the inadequate name: stonecutter.

Then a further ten minutes to The Mall, just past the
cinema where the anvil bells
of the glowing forge rang out and Joe Connolly
coaxed crude metal
into intricate shapes as if it were the plasticine of his
hand and brain co-ordination.
This was design by doing, as customers imagined
aloud what they desired in practice
by discussing the number of twirls and leaves they
would like to grace their gates. There the intricate
balance between imagination and reality was forged.
Joe's work adorned and secured many an entrance
and exit
even the convent had its boundaries set by him.

Then on to the Ballygaddy Road, a place of many
talents
and where the dressmaker Mrs Flaherty toiled in her
house-cum-workshop.
Armed to the teeth with pins in her lips in readiness
for fixing
she employed skills that defined the bespoke and
were evident in each measurement and scissor cut.
A huge iron, retrieved from the open fire, hissed
trainlike as it folded
and flattened the willing material on a room-dwarfing
table.

Her level playing field in an unfair world.
There, flat materials would be formed to caress that
extraordinary variety
of three dimensional contours that is the human body.
Whether for a two piece suit, a wedding dress or a
ballgown, her fine feathers made fine birds.
What home in MacHale Terrace did not boast at least
one garment fashioned by Mrs Flaherty?
She could metamorphise a mother's wedding dress
into a confirmation gown for her daughter
then a first communion dress for her youngest.

But a few paces away, stood the workshop of the
O'Rourke carpenters
where doors were custom made of well discussed,
highly figured and seasoned wood.
Each would fit snugly into an existing frame however
skewed –
a one-off fitted to perfection in an irregular world, not
some tolerated item imposing itself.
This respected artefact would be visited three months
later to ensure that it had settled in
with careful final adjustment to make it gently clonk
close on the inner and outer worlds
— a threshold of tension between the public and private
domains.
And just visible tall upright threatening, lurking in the
workshop corner, two coffins
Handcrafted reminders of our mortality.

Where to stop in this Hermitage of treasures? Perhaps
at Paddy Donoghue's,
whose hand stitched, brass embellished harnesses set
off many a fine horse,
or famed footballer Frank son of Jim Stockwell
whose shop signs with letters

defiantly stood proud of their flat surface;
Why not the bakers Clorans and Lydons where ovens
were fired up at around 4am
or Bob Holmes barber and provider of apprenticeships?

Not forgetting the Walsh brothers — a quartet of tailoring talents
three in Tuam and Richard in Kilcreevanty
or the Holian family of plasterers, bricklayers and builders.
Or Tommy Acton the bonesetter 'with the gift' in Desmesne cottages.

And precious to me are the cherished youthful
memories of dad's workshop
where I learned to anneal copper and temper steel
and that mecca of skills orchestrated by Franz Kaplan
in the workshop of the sugar factory
or…… an ever growing repertoire limited only by our
own lack of insight.

Mike Cooley

This poem was first published in AI & Society *Vol.28 No.4 Dec 2013*

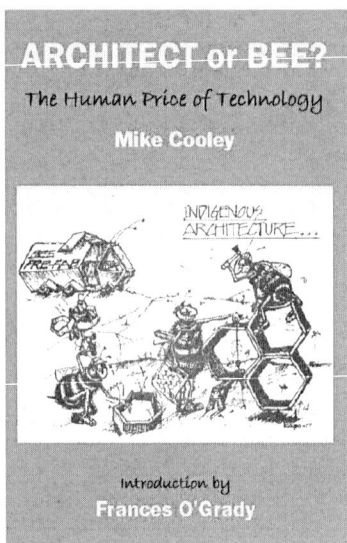